Anonymous

World's Fair. Jamaica at Chicago.

An account descriptive of the colony of Jamaica, with historical and other

appendices. Vol. 1

Anonymous

World's Fair. Jamaica at Chicago.
An account descriptive of the colony of Jamaica, with historical and other appendices. Vol. 1

ISBN/EAN: 9783337325329

Printed in Europe, USA, Canada, Australia, Japan

Cover: Foto ©Andreas Hilbeck / pixelio.de

More available books at **www.hansebooks.com**

WORLD'S FAIR.

–○–▣–○–

Jamaica at Chicago.

–○–▣–○–

AN ACCOUNT DESCRIPTIVE OF THE

COLONY OF JAMAICA,

WITH HISTORICAL AND OTHER APPENDICES.

–○–▣–○–

Compiled under the direction of

Lt. Col. the Hon. C. J. WARD, C. M. G.

Honorary Commissioner for Jamaica.

❧

NEW YORK:
WM. J. PELL, PRINTER, 92 JOHN STREET.

1893.

Respectfully Dedicated

to

His Excellency Sir Henry A. Blake, K. C. M. G.,

Governor of Jamaica.

To His Excellency Sir H. A. Blake, K. C. M. G.,

Sir:

In asking you to permit me to associate your name with this little hand=book which I have had prepared for free distribution at the Chicago Exhibition, I am prompted by the recollection of what you have done, so zealously and at the same time so unassumingly, in giving promi= nence to Jamaica as a possibly unequalled health resort and as a profitable field of settlement for would=be British Colonists or United States citizens, seeking a home under the British flag.

With politics I, as Commissioner for Jamaica, have nothing to do, but I think I am justified in availing myself, on behalf of my fellow= colonists, of this opportunity of expressing to Your Excellency the gratification felt by all Jamaicans at the sincere and hearty manner in which you have interested yourself in all that interests us, in which you have cordially thrown yourself into our lives and become one of us in your endeavours, since your assumption of the government of this colony, to do all in your power to promote, socially, morally and commercially, the best and highest interests of this ancient and loyal colony.

I am, Sir,

CHARLES J. WARD.

Kingston, Jamaica,
March, 1893.

CONTENTS.

DESCRIPTIVE ACCOUNT OF THE PARISHES
OF JAMAICA.

THE Island of Jamaica is essentially the most important of the British West Indian Islands, not only on account of its greater size, but also by reason of the varied beauty of its scenery, the capabilities of its soil and the healthiness of its climate. Less than a century ago, large fortunes were made in Jamaica and money was spent wildly, lavishly and often riotously. Subsequently, after the emancipation of the slaves, it settled down into quietude, and there were those who spoke of its palmy days as past, never to return. Lately, however, Jamaica has undoubtedly experienced a revival of popularity and of prosperity, a result largely due to intelligent enterprise and industry. It is not intended that these pages shall be filled to any extent with statistics, but, as evidence of the truth of the statement made in the previous sentence, it may be noted that the value of the fruit exported in 1879 was £40,166, and in 1892 it had risen to £315,000. So, too, with the educational and social condition of the people, much as there is still to be done and to be undone, to be learned and to be unlearned, there are on all sides, plainly visible, signs of progress and advancement, healthy signs, too, of a progress which has only just begun, but which will not stop until it reaches permanent prosperity. Another change, too, has come over Jamaica. It has long since ceased to be a yellow-fever bed and the favoured camping-ground of malaria. The growth of medical knowledge, and of sanitary science, and the application of common sense, and the lessons of daily experience have proved that life may be lived healthily, usefully, actively, enjoyably in Jamaica as well as in any other part of the world. There is work that can be done by those who can, or must work. There is enough sport to attract the sportsman, who is not ambitious after big game. There is a wealth of flowers, ferns and foliage, of tropical and sub-tropical vegetable life. If art has done little, nature has done much to allure and attract those who seek ease and enjoyment. The genial warmth of the plains will prolong the life of the consumptive, while on the hills can be found air as bracing and breezes as invigorating as any that can be found in more well-known health resorts.

The visitor to Jamaica sees much that is externally beautiful and historically interesting before the ship which brings him to this fair Island is anchored alongside one of the wharves, which line the northern shore of Kingston harbour. From the time when the Blue Mountain range comes into view and the steamer passes the Morant Point Lighthouse, the traveller, within one or two weeks of snow and damp, and warm overcoats and fur-lined gloves, can lounge on deck and feast his eyes on a succession of scenes as picturesque and as dazzling in their beauty and varied charms as are to be seen anywhere in or out of the tropics.   There are the rock-bound shore, the level beach, plains running down to the sea, gloomy lagoons and thick jungles of vegetable growth, broken here and there by river courses or dry ravines, while in the back-ground are to be seen mountains and hills differing in height from the modest hillock by the beach to the stately Blue Mountain Peak in the distant centre of the Island, the whole covered either with careful cultivation or with the reckless luxuriance of tropical life.   Passing Morant Bay, the scene of the unhappy disturbances in 1865, he catches a glimpse of sugar estates, notable among which is that of Albion, with its waving sugar-canes, its feathery palms, its little Coolie colony;

A BIT OF KINGSTON HARBOUR.

of the quaintly-shaped Sugar-Loaf Hill, whence a pilot is wont to come on board; of the remains of an old Spanish fortification, after which he soon reaches the narrow neck of land which runs for some four or five miles parallel to the shore on which stands the City of Kingston and which makes the Kingston harbour one of the safest and most splendid in the world.   About midway on this neck of land—called the Palisades or Palisadoes—is Plumb Point Lighthouse and at the western extremity is situated the town of Port Royal.   Rounding Port Royal the steamer sails across the harbour and pulls up alongside its wharf in Kingston.

The City of Kingston has had an exciting and eventful history.   Many of the survivors of the 1692 earthquake at Port Royal settled on the sea-board of the Liguanea plain, and Kingston is the gradual out-growth of that settlement.   Its progress, though slow at first, was accelerated in 1703 by a fire which completely destroyed the revived Port Royal and which drove many of the unfortunate inhabitants of the latter town to try their fortunes in Kingston.

If, however, Kingston owed its origin to the misfortunes of Port Royal, it has not been without its own share of troubles. Earthquake and hurricane have done their dire work at times, but fire has been Kingston's most persistent foe, the years 1780, 1843, 1862 and 1882 being the most calamitous. Bearing in mind then that for more than half a century—we may almost say for more than a century—no generation of Kingstonians has been without its recollection of devastating, destructive fire, it is not to be wondered at that the city, as it now stands, presents few features of architectural interest and contains few buildings of magnificent proportions. The city is constructed after the chess-board fashion of modern cities, the streets and lanes being parallel, or at right angles, to each other. In the centre of the city is the Kingston Parade Garden, a square of ten acres, neatly, but somewhat profusely, laid out with shade-giving and ornamental trees, many of which are interesting to botanists, and novel and curious to visitors from colder climes. The Gardens contain fountains and tanks where may be seen choice specimens of water lilies and other aquatic plants, and they are tolerably supplied with lounging seats.

Architecturally, the most striking building in Kingston is the Mico Institution. The story of the foundation of this Institution takes us back into the regions of romance two hundred years ago. There lived at that time a widow lady, whose husband, Sir Samuel Mico, had been Lord Mayor of London. A niece of Lady Mico lived with her as companion and was engaged to be married to a nephew of Lady Mico, who had promised to settle £2,000 on the couple when they were married. The marriage, however, did not take place, the lady preferring to run away with a military officer, and the £2,000 remaining in Lady Mico's possession. While these events were going on and some years afterwards, a good deal of excitement and indignation prevailed in England at the treatment which Christian captives received at the hands of Algerian pirates who kidnapped them and made them work as slaves. Among the sympathisers with these unhappy persons was Lady Mico, in whose will may be read the following words—"Whare as I gave Samuel Mico two thousand pounde when he had married one of my neeces but not performeing it I give one of the said thousand pounde to redeeme poor slaves which I would have put out as my executrix think be the best for a yearly revenew to redeem some yearly." Before this bequest was available by Lady Mico's death, Algerian piracy had been suppressed and its victims had been released. The money was invested by Order of the Court of Chancery in freehold property in London which so increased in value that in 1834 the Trust was worth more than £120,000. Suggestions as to the appropriation of this money had been made from time to time, but nothing was done until in the year above-mentioned (1834,) at the instigation of Sir Thomas Fowell Buxton, it was decided that it might be legitimately devoted to the Christian undenominational education of West Indian children. The Mico Institution in Hanover Street, Kingston, is one of the consequences of this decision. It consists of a handsome and substantial block of buildings, containing a Training College for upwards of fifty resident students in preparation for the profession of school-master and a day-school for 300 pupils.

The Kingston Markets are well worth a visit.   Here may be seen turtle, meat, poultry, fish, many of which are remarkable for the startling beauty of their colour, together with heaps of tropical fruits and vegetables, brought down overnight, mainly on women's heads, from distant parts of the Island.   The noise, the bustle, the clatter of tongues, the seeming confusion, the spontaneous out-flow of good nature all combine to make a visit to a Kingston market, especially on Saturday morning, a sight and a scene which will not readily be forgotten.   Of the two Kingston markets the Victoria Market is situated at the southern end

STREET VIEW, KINGSTON.

of King Street, and may be reached by tram from almost any part of the city. It is a handsome and spacious building, conveniently arranged both for purchasers and ' for sellers, within a few yards of the public landing-place on the North-shore of the harbour, and therefore exposed to the refreshing sea-breeze which cools the heated town.   The other market is to the west of the Parade Gardens, and was built in 1887, and called the Jubilee Market in commemoration of the fiftieth year of the Queen's Accession.

The Court House in Harbour Street, though externally unlovely, is not without its points of interest.   Persons accustomed to the small and badly-ventilated English Courts will be pleasantly surprised at the dimensions of the Jamaica Court-room.   On the walls of the Court House are two striking and well-executed paintings of Sir Joshua Rowe and Sir Bryan Edwards, two former dispensers of justice in the colony.

In the same building are situated the offices of the Registrar and the Supreme Court Library, together with the offices assigned to other officials connected with the administration of the law. The Library, in addition to a valuable collection of law reports, contains several documents of more than ordinary interest. Many ancient documents were destroyed by the earthquake of 1692, after which date the higher Courts were held either at Spanish Town or at Kingston. There is, however, at the Court House the register of the Chancellor's Court at Port Royal containing an entry to the effect that news having reached Port Royal announcing the death of His Majesty, Charles II., and the accession to the throne of His Royal Highness the Duke of York and Albany under the name of James II., the Court would adjourn for two weeks. But the greatest curiosity of all is a bundle of papers which have a history stranger than the most far-fetched conception of the most imaginative writer of fiction. In the year 1799 the brig " Nancy " was captured by the British cutter " Sparrow " and brought into Port Royal, the officers and crew being on trial in the Kingston Vice-Admiralty Court for piracy. No papers were found on the " Nancy," and for want of evidence which they would have supplied, the prosecution was on the point of breaking down. About this time the man-of-war " Abergavenny " was anchored off Jacmel, in Haiti, and the officers were serving their country by fishing for sharks. One of these sharks being caught, the sailors cut it open and in its belly was found a bundle of papers. Sailing for Kingston soon after, the bundle of papers was sent on shore by the captain who knew nothing of the capture of the " Nancy." They arrived while the trial for piracy was going on, and on investigation, were found to be the missing papers of the " Nancy," which had been thrown overboard to prevent their being used, and which were presented in Court in time to be used for securing the conviction and subsequent hanging of the crew of pirates.

The Institute of Jamaica in East Street is both a Museum and a Library. Unfortunately, it is too small for its purposes, and consequently its usefulness is somewhat interfered with. The Library is well stocked with standard books and contains a really valuable collection of books and pamphlets bearing on the history and natural productions of the West Indies. A Portrait Gallery of Jamaican celebrities is being gradually made complete, and lectures on literary and scientific subjects are frequently given. Like the Library, the Museum suffers from its insufficient size. It contains, however, many objects of much interest which well repay inspection. Among these is a collection illustrative of the geology of the Island, made by the officers of the Geological Survey between the years 1860 and 1866. A collection of specimens of Jamaica woods fills one small room. The herbarium contains complete sets of the ferns, the grasses, the sedges, and the orchids of Jamaica. There are also well-preserved specimens of the shells, fishes, birds, reptiles and insects of the island. The archæological section contains curious relics of the Indian population disturbed by Columbus and exterminated by the Spaniards, the bell of the old Port Royal Church submerged by the 1692 earthquake and subsequently rescued by divers, and also one of the old iron cages in which in days gone by criminals were enclosed and suspended on trees to die of exposure and starvation.

The Women's Self-help Society, apart from the philanthropic purposes for which it was founded and which it serves, is well stocked with fans, d'oyleys and other articles gracefully designed and carefully executed. Its premises in Church are conveniently situated and may reasonably be considered a small museum of works of art and taste.

Various religious sects have their places of worship in Kingston, but none of them claim to be grand or great specimens of ecclesiastical architecture. The Presbyterian Kirk in East Queen Street and the Wesleyan Chapel adjoining it, and known as the Coke Chapel, in memory of Dr. Coke, an eminent and honored Methodist missionary a hundred years ago, are perhaps the best and most complete to look at. The Roman Catholic Church, or pro-cathedral, is undergoing enlargement and, when finished, will be a handsome structure.

KINGSTON FROM HARBOUR.

Almost opposite to this last-named building is a striking and ornate Jewish Synagogue. The first place, however, must be given to the old Kingston Parish Church, the bright and cheerful interior of which atones for its somewhat sombre exterior. Within the walls of the Parish Church and near the communion rails, are buried all that could perish of Admiral Benbow, who died in Kingston in the year 1702.

Until within the last few years, the insufficiency of hotel and boarding accommodation was a great drawback in Kingston. Any ground for complaint of this sort has to a great extent been removed. In addition to numerous boarding-houses, most of which are clean and comfortable, and the most prominent of which is at Park Lodge and at Streadwick's Marine Gardens, there are substantially-built and fully-equipped hotels at Myrtle Bank, on the northern shore of the Harbour, in Heywood Street in the centre of the city, and at Constant Spring in the neighbouring parish of St. Andrew, about six miles from Kingston, with which it is connected by tram-lines. Both Myrtle Bank and Constant Spring hotels are spacious and well-conducted establishments. The former is almost in the centre of the business portion of Kingston, while the latter is removed from the heat and glare of the streets of a tropical town. In addition to the ordinary conveniences of hotels, both Myrtle Bank and Constant Spring are provided with large swimming baths.

Kingston also possesses its theatre, its race course, its clubs, some connected with sport, others existing for social purposes. The Jamaica Club in Hanover Street always welcomes strangers heartily; the Royal Jamaica Yacht Club has commodious quarters in the east of the city; the Society of Agriculture and Commerce has its home in Harbour Street, and its table is well supplied with the latest English and American papers.

The small, but once wealthy and important town of Port Royal stands at the Western extremity of the narrow peninsula, called the Palisades which separates Kingston Harbour from the open sea. Looking at Port Royal at the present day it is difficult to understand how it could once have deserved the description of being "the finest town in the West Indies and at that time the richest spot in the universe." Earthquake, fire and storm have done their work on the town and more peaceful ways and customs have put a stop to buccaneering and other means of acquiring unlawful wealth. The greatest calamity which has ever befallen Port Royal was the earthquake on the 17th of June, 1692, which submerged the greater part of the town. This dreadful event has often been described, or perhaps we should say that a description of it written by the clergyman at Port Royal, who was among the survivors of the earthquake, has often been quoted and adapted by subsequent historians and writers. The following extract from the Hand-book of Jamaica summarises the terrible catastrophe :—

"Whole streets with their inhabitants were swallowed up by the opening of the earth, which when shut upon them squeezed the people to death, and in that manner several were left with their heads above ground and others covered with dust and earth by the people who remained in the place. It was a sad sight to see the harbour covered with dead bodies of people of all conditions, floating up and down without burial, for the burying place was destroyed by the earthquake, which dashed to pieces tombs and the sea washed the carcases of those who had been buried out of their graves." At Green Bay there is still the tomb of Lewis Galdy, "who was swallowed up by the earthquake and by the Providence of God was, by another shock, thrown into the sea and miraculously saved by swimming until a boat took him up. He lived many years after in great reputation, beloved by all who knew him and much lamented at his death." The ruins of old Port Royal are even yet visible in clear weather from the surface of the waters under which they lie and relics are often procured by divers on exploring the ruins.

The greater part of the present town of Port Royal is occupied by the quarters of the naval and military troops, and by batteries and other means of defence. It is reached from Kingston by steam launch or by other boats.

To the North of Kingston is the Parish of

ST. ANDREW,

the lower portion of which may be regarded as a suburb of Kingston, for here, within easy reach of office or store, are the homes of many of the leading commercial and professional men.

The tram-car from the Victoria Market terminus runs in a northerly direction about seven and one-half miles from Kingston, passing through the pretty

CONSTANT SPRING HOTEL, KINGSTON.

village of Halfway-Tree and stopping at Constant Spring. Halfway-Tree has its Court House and Market and a beautifully restored Parish Church, which is quite worth seeing as a model of what can be done by good taste and religious devotion. The central East window of the Church is a memorial of Dr. Aubrey Spencer, second Bishop of Jamaica. In the middle is a representation of the Ascension of Jesus Christ, on either side of which are side lights, that on the right depicting tropical scenery suggestive of the Bishop's connection with Jamaica, and that on the left showing an Arctic scene commemorative of his occupancy of the See of Newfoundland from which he was translated to Jamaica. To the North of this middle window, and also at the East end, is a window in memory of Dr. Charles Campbell, a late doctor in Kingston, equally renowned for his philanthropy and his professional skill; this window appropriately contains representations of St. Luke, the Medico-Evangelist, the Healing of the Paralytic and the Good Samaritan. The corresponding window on the South perpetuates the memory of the piety and good works of the Doctor's brother, the late Venerable Archdeacon Campbell, and represents the Adoration of the Magi, the Resurrection and the Washing the Disciples' Feet. Monuments and memorial tablets of departed Governors and local celebrities are to be found both in the Church and in the church-yard. Passing the Constant Spring Hotel which has already been mentioned, we come to the foot of Stony Hill. At the top of Stony Hill we are 1,425 feet above the level of the sea, and the difference of climate between it and the lowlands is very perceptible, though the distance between the summit of the hill and Kingston is only nine miles. Here is the private residence of the present Bishop of Jamaica and a block of buildings which were formerly the military encampment for white troops, but which are now the premises of the Government Reformatory for boys. Beyond Stony Hill to the left hand side of the road, we soon reach a wide stretch of land, devoted to the culti-vation of tobacco and largely inhabited by Cubans; this tobacco has a very high reputation, and there are not wanting connoisseurs who prefer it to the choicest brands of Cuban growth. On certain days, and under atmospheric conditions, during the curing season the traveller, journeying from Kingston across the Island, may inhale for some considerable time the unadulterated flavour of the finest tobacco. The road—which is known as the Junction Road—then continues down hill till it reaches the confines of the Parish of St. Mary and terminates at the little sea-port town of Annotto Bay. On this road, nineteen miles from Kingston and eleven miles from Annotto Bay, are the Castleton Gardens. Castleton is in St. Mary's Parish, but on account of its accessibility to Kingston and St. Andrew is more properly mentioned here. A double buggy from Kingston to the Gardens and back can be hired for 30s. These Gardens contain a large collection of native and tropical plants. and no one ought to leave Jamaica without visiting them. Their chief features are the palmetum, a collection of economic, spice and fruit trees, a fine collec-tion of East Indian and West Indian orchids, an experimental ground for new industrial plants, and large nurseries containing cacao, rubber plants, nutmeg, clove, peppers, mango, vanilla, cardamum, sarsaparilla, Liberian coffee, etc., etc. Apart from industrial plants, Castleton Gardens contain such interesting Botanical specimens as, among others, the splendid Victoria Regia (the Water Lily of the Amazon), the Amherstia Nobilis, the most magnificent of ornamental flowering trees, the Java Upas Tree, the Ravenalia Madagascariense, commonly known as the Traveller's Tree of Madagascar, a tree from which a cold drink can be extracted at any minute the whole year round. Alongside the Eastern boundary of the Gardens flows the Wag Water River, on the Western bank of which is a grotto, convenient for picnic parties, shaded by the foliage of trees and protected by overhanging rocks. The average annual rainfall at Castleton is more than 108 inches and therefore, on the occasion of a visit there, it is wise to be provided with umbrellas and waterproofs.

Another road from Kingston is that which leads through Gordon Town to Newcastle and the St. Andrew's Hills.   Passing the Jamaica High School for boys, the University College and the Hope Gardens, a newly founded Government Institution, the road plunges into a gorge that is thoroughly characteristic of Jamaica mountain scenery.   On the one hand a precipitous bank of ferns and wild-flowers and patches of guinea grass, now and then a boulder of dark grey rock cropping out, with sheltering clumps of moss and fern in its niches and hollows.   On the other hand, a hundred feet below, the Hope River roars along over its bed of smooth boulders and brown gravel.   The road winds sharply in and out, following the contour of the hills, and guarded at nearly every

PORT ROYAL.

turn by strong retaining walls from the dangers of the precipice that overhangs the river.   Higher and higher it mounts; cottages dot the hillside; ferns and begonias cluster thicker; the air is fresher and more bracing and our spirits rise involuntarily.   Then after an hour's brisk drive from Kingston the village of Gordon Town is reached, where there is just enough room for a straggling row of houses between the mountain at the back and the river at the foot of the precipice in front.

Beyond Gordon Town progress must be made either on foot or on horseback, the mountain track being too narrow and too steep for buggy or carriage.

Reaching Newcastle and looking southward the visitor will be rewarded for his climb with a magnificent view of the Liguanea Plain, the Town and Harbour of Kingston, and the sea beyond to a far horizon; while to the north, east and west, tower the slopes and crests of the Blue Mountains. A walk along any of the numerous paths across the slopes and leading to the ridges above will repay him with an endless wealth of ferns, orchids and wild flowers, and he will be reminded of home by the wild strawberries nestling in the hollows along the banks.

The highest point of this range is the Blue Mountain Peak, 7,500 feet above sea level, the journey to which should be a two days' trip, spending the night in the hut on the top of the Peak. Provisions will have to be laid in, and guides can be procured who will also act as porters.

The road mounts ridge after ridge, winding down steep mountain sides, crossing the streams that rush down every gorge, skirting along the slopes and mounting over the tops of the intervening hills, and now and then leaving one valley and following the course of another.

An easy ride of about four hours brings us to Farm Hill Coffee Plantation, where the keys of the hut on the Summit of the Peak and useful information about the road, or the weather, or the water supply may be obtained.

Leaving Farm Hill the road winds along past Whitfield Hall to Abbey Green, whose houses and terraces of solid masonry are perched on slopes of such surpassing steepness that they appear in imminent danger of tumbling headlong into the abyss that lies beneath them.

Behind this the road zig-zags up the steep side of the mountain, threading its course between fields of coffee, some of them of such venerable age that many of the coffee bushes have assumed the appearance of dwarfed trees from the constant lopping and priming, with trunks from six to nine inches in diameter, and a height of only four feet or thereabout.

The leaves of the Cinchona, blotched with scarlet, now add their quota of colour to the scene ; for we are leaving the coffee region behind and entering upon the elevation at which this useful febrifuge best flourishes. Hundreds of acres were planted here some fifteen years ago, and should have been a mine of wealth to the growers; but, now that artificial quinine can be produced so cheaply, the Cinchona plant runs wild and self-sown, growing in rank thickets on many a misty slope of the Blue Mountain.

On reaching the top, about two hours after leaving Farm Hill, we find a small open space covered with short springy turf and fringed with stunted trees. At one side of it stands a little hut of two rooms, where accommodations for the night may be had. There is a stove and a supply of firewood, which you may use, provided you replace the latter on leaving—a most rigidly observed point of Peak etiquette. To the south of the hut there is a narrow track leading down a precipitous ravine, near which is a small pool of water sufficient for one's absolute needs. Should the weather however have been abnormally dry this may fail, and in such seasons the wise traveller will bring drinking water with him.

The thermometer at early morning is frequently down to forty degrees Fahrenheit; on a recent occasion, during the cold wave of February, 1886, solid ice was found there.

The weather should of course be carefully considered, as on that depends entirely the success of the expedition; and it should be remembered that the annual rainfall at the Peak amounts to about 130 inches. The calm, clear weather prevailing about the time of the vernal and autumnal equinoxes will be found the most favourable for the ascent.

Other places of interest in the Parish of St. Andrew are the King's House, the official residence of the Governor, the grounds of which are beautifully laid out, and the Up-Park Camp Barracks, about one and one-half miles north of Kingston, the head-quarters of the West Indian Regiment. The military band plays once a week' in the evening and occasionally in the afternoon, and the Camp is a favourite resort for lovers of music.

KING'S HOUSE, SPANISH TOWN.

To the east of Kingston is the Parish of

ST. THOMAS.

For any one who has time to drive round the Island and to see what of Jamaica can be seen in a flying visit, a leisurely journey along the main coast road of the Island is an enjoyable experience. There are varieties of scenery, life, character; there are good roads and entertainments varying from good to moderate. To take this tour is perhaps the best way of seeing Jamaica, to follow its track may be the best way of illustrating and describing Jamaica. Let us start in an easterly direction from Kingston and drive in turn through the country parishes.

Kingston is soon left behind, the road passing between rows of detached villas, each with its garden bright with roses, and crotons and tropical flowers which bloom so brightly and luxuriantly that one can almost fancy they enjoy the pleasure of existence. Soon we are by the shore of the harbour and pass Rock Fort and Brighton Beach and the Head of the Harbour. Rock Fort is picturesque to look at, but obsolete and useless as a means of defence against modern artillery.

After about an hour's drive the Falls River is reached. There is, however, no river to be seen, but the dry bed of a water-course fringed with unsightly bush, mostly of a thorny description. But those who are equal to the task of leaving their buggy and walking a mile or so up the ravine to where it emerges from those volcanic rocks that frown down upon it, will find a stream of crystal water. Following the rocky path cut along one side of it they arrive at the foot of a romantic looking waterfall, roaring down a cañon whose adamant walls tower hundreds of feet above.

H. M. S. "URGENT."

This spot and its neighbourhood are historically interesting as having been the haunt, about one hundred and twenty years ago, of Three-Fingered Jack, whose exploits have found their way into English melodrama. He was a notorious negro highwayman, for dread of whom travellers refrained from passing along this road after dark. A price was set by the Government upon his head, and the reward was earned by a Maroon, who killed him and brought into Head-quarters the deformed hand that gave the robber his appellation, as proof positive of his achievement.

Leaving the Falls River the road crosses the spurs of the Blue Mountain Range that here fall abruptly into the sea. From the summits of some of these, as the road swings sharply round the head of a ravine, exquisite little glimpses are obtained between the hills of Port Royal, the Palisades, Kingston Harbour, and the distant heights beyond, with deep blue water in the foreground studded with the white sails of coasting vessels or fishing canoes.

And so on down the steep Four Mile Wood Hill and along the edge of a
mangrove swamp, until Albion Estate is reached, the bright green of whose rustling cane fields forms a pleasing contrast to the sombre tone of the forest
vegetation.   A few miles beyond Albion is the village of Yallahs, the principal
object of interest in which is the old church, the first erected on the Island after
its occupation by the English.   It is solidly built, but simple and unpretentious
in architecture.

About a mile and a half beyond Yallahs the Salt Ponds are reached, sheets
of stagnant brackish water, teeming with fish and swarming with alligators, of
which latter the traveller is sure to see one or two floating with snout and tail

CASTLETON GARDENS.

projecting above the surface of the water at almost any time of the day.   Passing
these, the scenery, which, but for the bold and ever changing outline of the hills
on the north, is rather monotonous, begins to improve.

We pass through one or two villages, with tall and graceful cocoanut palms
and fruit trees overshading the thatched huts, and knots of happy little
urchins playing by the roadside.   Crimson poinsettia and flowering hybiscus
brighten the hedges; and soon we approach the sea-shore again, along which
we skirt for nearly four miles, while on the left springs of fresh water gush
out of the rocks, and at one spot a waterfall comes tumbling into the road.

Now, the laughter of women and children rings out, bathing or washing
clothes in the stream, or filling their cans and calabashes with water.   Then a
stretch of wide common opens up dotted with browsing sheep and cattle, houses

and estates; buildings stand out against the background of the beautiful hills, and Belvidere Estate is passed, the original owner of which was Robert Freeman, the first Speaker of the first House of Assembly in Jamaica.

Passing through a forest of bananas, we come out into the course of the Morant River, where the many tracks that the water has torn up are bordered by beds of wild cane waving their silken plumes. Here and there a massive trunk, torn from the forest higher up, lies prostrate, witness of the fury of the swollen torrent. Looking up Northwards are to be seen the encircling sweep of the hills, and the Peaks of the Blue Mountains towering over all.

A mile beyond this is the town of Morant Bay, which has an unenviable notoriety as being the seat of the disturbances of 1865. Here one's attention is attracted by the sign of American enterprise in the wharf and buildings of the Boston Fruit Co., whose business has an important branch here. The Court House and the Square are objects of melancholy interest, the former being built upon the foundations of the old building destroyed by the rioters in 1865, while the square was the scene of much of the punishment that accompanied the retribution.

A visit to Morant Bay will not be complete without a run up the Blue Mountain Valley, one of the most charming bits of scenery to be found in the whole Island of Jamaica, as far as Serge Island Estate. This place will be found to combine the highest class of cane cultivation with the most improved methods of sugar manufacture; while its red-roofed " great house " is a fine specimen of old Jamaica architecture. Add to these a beautiful and tastefully laid out garden, where tropical plants and those of more temperate regions are made to grow side by side in bewildering variety, surrounded by a wealth of ferns and orchids, and you have a perfectly ideal tropical demesne, even without the incomparable background of bold forest-clad mountain range and towering peaks in which it nestles.

Seven miles beyond Morant Bay is situated the shipping place of Port Morant. Town, properly speaking, there is none, in spite of the safe and almost land-locked harbour. But considerable business is done here in the fruit trade, this being the head-quarters on the south side of the Island of the Boston Fruit Co. Their wharves and offices are at the east side of the harbour, where the depth is great enough for steamers of 2,000 tons to moor alongside in perfectly smooth water. Along the road hither, if it be the day of the arrival of a fruit steamer, will be met spring carts and wagons, all laden with the luscious banana.

The road now leaves the coast and turns toward the little town of Bath. The scenery becomes more and more tropical and the vegetation richer and richer. Gorgeous shrubs line the roadside, the ever frequent stream is crossed, now by bridge, now by ford, now small, now large, until we reach the Plantain Garden River, which, rising far away in the recesses of the Blue Mountains, flows from west to east, and discharges itself into the sea at Holland Bay to the north of the Morant Point Lighthouse. It traverses in its course a plain bounded on the north by the precipitous slope of the Blake Mountains—until recently known as the John Crow Mountains—and on the south by a range of low hills which divide it from the sea on that side. This plain

it covers, when in flood, with alluvial deposit from the hills above, thus
making the Plantain Garden River district one of the most fertile spots on
the Island.

About a quarter of a mile further, after fording a tributary of the Plantain Garden River, we find ourselves at a sudden turn of the road in the
town of Bath, the approach to which is by an avenue in which Otaheite
apple trees predominate, interspersed with ackees, mangoes and cotton trees.

The glory has departed from Bath, as from many another Jamaica town. But
the mineral waters, to which it owes its existence, are still there. They are worth
visiting on account of the natural beauty of their situation, and the sufferer from

ON THE WAG WATER AT CASTLETON.

rheumatism, or any ailment of a cutaneous nature, will here find relief, if not
ultimate cure.

The way to them lies along a narrow gorge bordered with fern and moss and
creepers covering the dark grey rock and almost hiding from view the river rushing along below. Tree ferns spread abroad their arching fronds, and the air is
fragrant and heavy with moisture, for it is a veritable hot-house of nature. Sudden
showers of rain are apt to come pelting down, a danger which has been provided
against by the erection, at intervals of half a mile, of zinc-roofed sheds over the
road. From out the rocks above, tiny streamlets trickle across into the river
beneath, some hot, some cold, and high over all nods the graceful bamboo with
its whispering leaves. A mile and a half of this enchanted road brings us to the
Baths, which are wedged in between the hillside and the river bank. The springs

that supply them with hot and cold water bubble out of the rocks higher up within a few feet of each other, the hot one at a temperature of 130 degrees Fahrenheit. The following is the analysis of the water:

Chloride of Sodium,	13.84
Chloride of Potassium,	0.32
Sulphate of Calcium,	5.01
Sulphate of Soda,	6.37
Carbonate of Soda,	1.69
Silica,	2.72
Oxide of sodium, combined with silica,	1.00
Organic matter,	0.99

The above being the proportion to one gallon of water.

There is accommodation for visitors at Bath, but much requires to be done in the way of increasing and improving the accommodation, before the virtues of the mineral springs are as widely used and appreciated as they ought to be.

In the river, above the baths, are deep pools and foaming cascades of most exquisite beauty. The curative properties of the springs are said to have been accidentally discovered by a slave in the early part of the last century.

In the year 1774 a botanic garden was established at Bath, of which now only about an acre remains; sadly neglected, but containing some magnificent specimens of ornamental and economic trees transported hither from other lands. Here flourishes and flowers, although almost uprooted by hurricane, a solitary *Amherstia nobilis*. Great tangles of knotted vine, vanilla among them, clasp the branches of the *Spathodea* and *Barringtonia* in their embrace, forming a canopy under which palms, rattans, dracænas, irises and a legion of others rankly grow. But chief of all is the gigantic *coco de mer*, the palm that takes seventy years to arrive at maturity, and under any one leaf of which a dozen men could find perfect shelter from the heaviest shower of rain.

Leaving Bath we drive along a level road through the Plantain Garden River Plain, where banana cultivation is largely carried on.

It is a noble view that unfolds itself to the gaze, as, after a drive of six miles, the traveller begins the ascent of the Quaw Hill, and turning round sees this fruitful land stretched out below, banana fields alternating with pasture land, the tall chimneys and white works, relics of the by-gone sugar industry still standing among the broad leaves, teams of cattle toiling along before the plough, and the river here and there gleaming out from its fringe of rustling bamboos.

But this soon fades from sight, and, reaching the top of the hill we are presently on a breezy upland where the road is scarcely discernible, and the telegraph posts are almost the only guide across the short, crisp turf, sweetened by the spray flung over it by the incoming breakers from the open sea.

Passing the clean little town of Manchioneal, scene of some of the exploits recorded in "Tom Cringle's Log," embowered in cocoanut palms that grow down to the very edge of the land-locked little harbour, after a few miles of romantic scenery, a turn of the road reveals the east harbour of Port Antonio, the chief town in the Parish of

PORTLAND.

An outjutting promontory of coral rock, carpeted with green turf, divides the bay into two harbours. On this spit of land stands the picturesque remains of an ancient Fort, and behind it the old barracks. From the further margin of each harbour the hills rise step by step, profusely covered with tropical vegetation and plumed with many a tall cocoanut, among which the white walls and the green windows and the red roofs of the houses look out

ON THE ROAD TO CASTLETON.

seawards. Behind these again mount ridge upon ridge of the Blue Mountain Range right up into the clouds that hang round the Peaks. Outside the mouth of the harbour white-crested waves break against the iron rock on which the red lighthouse is perched. The vessel comes bounding in on the swell, rushing apparently to certain destruction, when, suddenly swinging under the lee of the Island that guards the mouth of the west harbour, she glides along on even keel over the unruffled surface of this harbour till she anchors alongside one of the wharves, where two or three steamers are generally to be seen taking in fruit for the American market.

For here are the head-quarters of the Boston Fruit Co., whose enterprise has, it may almost be said, saved the two most easterly parishes of the Island from reverting, sugar being extinct, to the condition of primeval forest. The American visitor might well fancy himself in some town in the Southern States in his native land—American vessels in the harbour, American boats scudding about the bay, and American wagons rattling along the street.

The head offices of the Boston Fruit Co. are at Long Wharf, Boston, Mass., and they despatch two steamers weekly thence and from Baltimore. Their vessels being primarily intended for the fruit trade, the passenger accommodation is necessarily limited ; but eight or ten can be carried conveniently at the very reasonable rates of $60.00 for a return ticket from Boston, and $50.00 from Baltimore. The passage is made in five and a half or six days.

If the tourist should choose this means of reaching Jamaica he will never forget the entrance to Port Antonio Harbour, especially if he should chance to arrive at early morning or towards sunset.

Among the places of interest to be visited in the neighbourhood the magnificent banana plantations at Golden Vale and Seaman's Valley are the chief. The effect of many hundred acres of broad shining leaves glistening in the sun, row upon row, with the virgin forest of the mountain ridges for a background, and the broad bosom of the Rio Grande, the second largest river in the Island, gleaming in front, cannot be surpassed anywhere.

From Port Antonio the route lies westward along the north coast of the Island, passing the little towns of Hope Bay and Buff Bay. Still roars the sea on the right, open bay giving place to quiet cove, and occasionally a bit of mangrove swamp, where the tall trees stand up on stilts of arched roots between which oozes sluggish black water. Myriads of queerly shaped crabs scurry across the road. They appear to have concentrated all their energies on the development of one enormous claw, which, carried defiantly across the face, wide open, is in absurd disproportion to the rest of the structure. These breaks in the chain only give one greater zest for the enjoyment of the next bit of coral beach and cocoanut-fringed emerald water.

And wherever cultivation is practicable there grow bananas. We pass also through two or three of the largest cocoanut plantations in the Island, and witness abundant signs of the importance of the banana and the cocoanut in the welfare of the population of this neighbourhood. If the tourist should happen to be thirsty by the way, he may do a great deal worse than try a water cocoanut. That means an unripe cocoanut, in which the meat is of such texture that it may be scooped out and eaten with a spoon—and the water of which has a most pleasingly palatable flavour. If it be early in the day, the temperature of this is sure to be several degrees lower than that of any other fluid that he is likely to be able to procure along the road.

The contemplated extension of the Jamaica railway as far as Port Antonio will, when effected, make the towns along this road independent of the weather, which now, during the " northern " season, often interferes very seriously with the fruit trade on account of the unprotected state of the harbours facing the north.

About eight miles beyond Buff Bay, the western boundary of the Parish of Portland is passed, and we enter the classic ground of

ST. MARY,

around which cluster a hundred memories of Columbus and the Spanish occupation.

The first town reached is Annotto Bay. the situation of which is suggestive of moisture and malaria, owing to the fact that three or four rivers here find their way into the sea. Judging, however. from official statistics. Annotto Bay is by no means so unhealthy as might be expected. It is a prosperous little town and a growing centre of the fruit trade.

ON THE ROAD TO GORDON TOWN.

Proceeding westward along the coast, Port Maria is reached—Port Maria, the probable Santa Gloria of Columbus. This is a flourishing town, with its Church, Court House and Hospital all in good order and in creditable condition. It has a fairly good harbour and has not been without its share of the banana prosperity. Near the Church is the Victoria Market. built in 1887, in commemoration of the Jubilee of the Queen's Accession. On a promontory, overlooking the harbour, is a building formerly known as Fort Haldane, from which a wide-reaching view on either side may be obtained, a view including the town and harbour, neighbouring estates with their varied cultivation together with Cabrietta Island. a reef which acts as a breakwater and protection to the harbour. The Fort is now devoted to more peaceful uses than its name implies, being the home of Gray's Charity, an almshouse where shelter and means of living are provided for a certain number of the poor of the Parish of St. Mary.

Some miles to the west of Port Maria is Oracabessa Bay, on the shores of which Christopher Columbus probably first landed in Jamaica on the fifth day of May, 1494. This interesting little place bears a good character as a health-resort and bananas are shipped from its safe little harbour. Beyond Oracabessa is Rio Nuevo, another place of note in the history of the Colony. It was here that the Spaniards, taking advantage of the distress and disorganization of the British troops, attempted to regain possession of the Island. On a rocky eminence near the sea at Rio Nuevo, Don Christopher Sasia, with upwards of 1,000 men, occupied what he considered an impregnable fortress. Here the Spaniards were attacked by the British and after a desperate fight were defeated with terrible loss of life.

At the north of this parish is Scott's Hall, one of the Maroon towns, not far from which is Job's Hill, where some valuable copper ore was found in 1852. An unsuccessful attempt to work a copper mine was made—the failure being due not to the absence of the mineral so much as to the employment of a wrong method of working.

The Parish of St. Mary is memorable in the history of Jamaica as having been the scene of a formidable outbreak among the slaves in the year 1760. The insurgents were under the command of two Africans, named Tackey and Jamaica, through whose veins ran the fierce Cormantyn blood, and the former of whom had held high rank in his native country before being exiled into slavery. On the evening of Easter Sunday a party of slaves marched into Port Maria and seized the almost unprotected fort and magazine, thereby obtaining possession of arms and ammunition. On the following day they were joined by bands of fellow-conspirators from neighbouring estates and marched towards the interior of the Island, plundering Heywood Hall, Esher and other estates and killing the white inhabitants. They retired for rest and safety to Ballard's Valley, where they began to enjoy, in wild revellings and reckless carousals, the fruits of a victory which was not as yet within their grasp. For their plot was revealed by one Yankee, who has been called "a faithful slave," a term which, while including faithfulness to his owner, certainly involves treachery to his comrades and fellow countrymen. The regular troops, the militia and hurriedly-enrolled volunteers were quickly on the track of the rebels who, after a desperate struggle, were defeated with much loss of life. Tackey himself was shot by a Maroon; of the other ring-leaders one was burnt and two were hung in chains, and a large number of the rank and file were transported to the Bay of Honduras.

Leaving Oracabessa, the road crosses the White River, and we enter the Parish of

ST. ANN,

the "Garden of Jamaica," the loveliness and charm of which have, time after time, proved to be beyond the power of the pen of historians, travellers and descriptive writers. Let us quote some of these:

First of all Peter Martyr, to whom we are indebted for so much information relative to the early settlement of these regions, and who is said to have resided in the Abbey of Sevilla Nueva in St. Ann, speaks of sending a household servant to "looke into ye affaires of my Paradisian Jamaica." Then ·Bryan Edwards says:—"When Columbus first discovered Jamaica he approached it on " the northside, and beholding that part of the country which now constitutes " the Parish of St. Ann, he was filled with delight and admiration at the " novelty, variety and beauty of the prospect."

But Hill, in his "Lights and Shadows of Jamaica History," rises above them all to the height of positive rhapsody. "Earth," he says, "has nothing more

GORDON TOWN.

" lovely than the pastures and pimento groves of St. Ann, nothing more enchant" ing than its hills and vales, delicious in . verdure and redolent with the " fragrance of spices. Embellished with wood and water, from the deep forests, " from whence the streams descend to the ocean in falls, the blue haze of the air " blends and harmonizes all into beauty."

And truly it is a fair country. Here is the home of the fragrant pimento, more generally known as allspice, Jamaica's unique and indigenous product. Silver stems, crowned with dark leaves of glossy green, they stand in groups on the gentle slopes, shading the velvety common or the breast-high luscious guinea grass, where browse the sleek cattle, or, satiated and recumbent, chew the cud. The scent of the ripe berries fills the drowsy air, lulled by the hum of the bee and the roar of the waterfall. Graceful clumps of woodland, spreading ceibas, scarlet-blotched broad-leaf, crown the crests of the undulating hills, where from one, steeper than its fellows, the limestone crags crop out.

White roads bounded by grey stone walls wind along the hollows, dipping into the crystal rivulets where the water-lily floats, and sweep up the hill-sides to the white mansions glancing through their curtains of trailing creeper. The bright magenta of the Bougainvillea, the creamy whiteness of the stephanotis, the pale pink of the coralina enfold these lovingly, and with many another, fling broadcast their brightness and their fragrance.

For a background to our view we have hitherto always had the rugged outline of some ridge or peak of the Blue Mountains clad in virgin forest ; but now we exchange these for rounded hills and swelling pastures. The broad estuaries of sluggish rivers, the mangrove swamps, the stony beds of mountain torrents give place to babbling streams of a purity that looks as though the flood could never defile it, now sweeping in a clear steady current right out to the bar in which the white breakers tumble, now shooting out over the cliff sheer down to the beach in a silvery cascade.

There is something weird and mysterious about the origin of these streams. They are cradled in the bosom of the earth, in the limestone strata far beneath the surface, fed by many a "sink-hole;" now coming out to bask in the light of day for a mile or two, then disappearing again until they emerge for the final plunge into the sea. One of these, the Roaring River, has created for itself a veritable fairy-land in its course which we cross on the road to St. Ann's Bay, after passing the village of Ocho Rios. The noise which warns us of our approach to it amply justi- fies the name of the stream. It finds its way into the sea by a score of different channels, each overhung by vegetation in such a way that your first impression is that it is only a temporary flow of water escaping from some dam above, and will presently cease. The main stream is spanned by a strong stone bridge, from which we look down upon a scene which makes us rub our eyes and look and look again. There is a clear pool, calm of surface, but flowing nevertheless with a strong current seaward, out of which apparently grow cabbage palms, banyans, ferns, vines, and other trees and plants innumer- able. Looking upward, if we scramble out upon the projecting roots that form a rough bridge, the stream mounts terrace upon terrace, each curtained with an irridescent veil of falling water, which almost seems to drip from the branches of the trees that form the foreground, growing up in mid-stream.

Leaving the buggy and walking along the path-way about a mile from the road, we are rewarded by the sight of the great Fall, one of the loveliest objects in a land of beautiful things.

St. Ann's Bay, the principal town in the parish, is a clean little town, with a harbour open to the north, outjutting wharves, a street parallel to the harbour connected by cross streets with another further away, in which lie the principal dry goods and hardware stores. There is a neat little church, and the public offices are striking buildings. Cocoanut palms wave everywhere, and vegetation crops out in every corner that is not constantly trodden by passing feet.

About a mile to the west of St. Ann's Bay was the site of the first Capital of the Island, Sevilla Nueva, or Sevilla d'Oro, founded by Don Juan d'Esquivel, the first Spanish Governor of Jamaica.   It was of large extent, and contained a Cathedral, a Monastery, a Theatre, and many Palaces. Owing to some cause of which no record has been left, it was abandoned and allowed to decay till scarcely a trace remains of the ancient city.

To the East of St. Ann's Bay is Don Christopher's Cove, so called from the fact that Columbus is reported, on the occasion of his last voyage to the West Indies, to have there stranded his two last crippled ships.   Another place of interest to students of the early history of Jamaica is Runaway Bay, about ten

SAVANNA-LA-MAR.

miles from St. Ann's Bay on the Northern coast of the Parish of St. Ann. Hence it was that Don Arnoldi Sasi, the last of the Spanish Governors, after a desperate struggle with Cromwell's troops, managed to make his escape to Cuba.   Dry Harbour, the Puerto Bueno of the Spaniards, is reached by road or by water from St. Ann's Bay.   It is mainly interesting for its historic associations and for its proximity to a remarkable cavern at a place called Cave Hall Pen.   This Cave is very long and contains two galleries which branch into grottoes and side aisles, from which there are stalagmites and stalactites of strange beauty.

South-east of St. Ann's Bay is the inland village of Moneague where, at an elevation of 950 feet above the sea-level, is a small hotel.   The charges at the Moneague are not excessive, the climate is fairly good, and lovers of picturesque scenery will not be disappointed if they spend a few days there.

The mountains of this district of St. Ann have, like so many other parts of Jamaica, their bloody legends of bygone days, which may be related here.

About the year 1770, there lived at Pedro Vale in this district, Louis Hutchinson, a notorious murderer. Hutchinson was a Scotchman by birth, whose feelings had been hardened and disposition brutalised by the sad fate of his father and sister. His father had been murdered by a military officer who afterwards first outraged, and then murdered, his sister. Hutchinson lived at a house called "Edinburgh Castle," which overlooked a narrow pass leading from the North to the South of the Island. Here, assisted by his slaves, and under cover of a thick logwood fence, he waylaid the unwary traveller, and for many years few persons escaped his unerring aim. His victims were often mutilated and dismembered before being cast into a gully to decay, or be washed to the sea by the mountain torrents. His last victim was a man named Callendar, the manager of a neigh-

MARTHA BRAE, FALMOUTH.

bouring estate. The story goes that Hutchinson would imprison infirm or sick persons in order to fatten them for the sacrifice, and that one unhappy creature so imprisoned was a witness of the murder of Callendar, contrived to escape and reported what he had seen to the authorities. Hutchinson, now that concealment was no longer possible, fled to Old Harbour and put out to sea in a small, open boat, but was arrested by a vessel sent in search of him by Admiral Lord Rodney. The number of his victims is unknown, but as many as forty-seven watches were found in his house. He was hung in Spanish Town on the 16th of March, 1773.

Brown's Town is an important inland town in this parish. It is a great centre of the produce trade, and at all hours of the day and night in certain seasons, drays and carts may be met loaded with the fragrant pimento and the aromatic coffee, toiling up towards the town, or returning laden with the various commodities and necessaries of life with which the stores there are so well supplied. A bright, clean, smart-looking little place is this. None of those squalid tumble-down shanties, that so often offend the eye in the coast towns, meet the gaze. It carries in its face an air of prosperity that is no mere pretence.

To the West of St. Ann's Parish is that of

TRELAWNY,

which derives its name from Governor Sir William Trelawny, who died in Jamaica in the year 1772, and its chief town, Falmouth, is the second in size in the whole Island. The most interesting way by which to approach Falmouth is by road from Brown's Town. It is not merely that the scenery through which the road passes equals in picturesqueness that of other parts of Jamaica, but the social conditions

ROARING RIVER.

which prevail differ from those of other districts. On the left is a district which some fifty years ago was made the scene of a curious experiment, namely, an attempt to introduce European immigrants into Jamaica. If in one sense the experiment was a failure, in another it was a success. For if on the one hand it showed that, as a general rule, the European constitution cannot stand prolonged out-door labour on the hot plains of Jamaica, on the other hand it proved that such labour was quite possible in the cool and healthy mountain districts. Unfortunately the experiment was mismanaged and ended disastrously. Many of these immigrants were German by nationality and were located in this part of Trelawny. Their descendents may be found in the neighbouring Ulster Spring district, where the percentage of crime and illegitimacy is less than in most other districts, and where the general condition is that of a happy and contented people. Falmouth itself is a neat, well-kept town, with broad streets and several handsome and substantial buildings. Foremost among these is the Court House. Trelawny has always been famed for the lavish hospitality of its inhabitants, and the receptions given to successive Governors at Falmouth are characteristic of this hospitality. On the walls of the Court House are mementoes of past Governors. One of these is a full length portrait of General Sir John Keene, who was Lieutenant Governor of the Colony from 1827-1829 and who, at a critical time, administered the Government with mingled firmness and conciliation. Another portrait here is that of Sir Charles Metcalfe, who was Governor from 1839 to 1842 and whose conduct, under circumstances of considerable difficulty, deservedly earned for him the respect and admiration of the colonists. The Episcopal Church at Falmouth is a fairly substantial building which is now being internally repaired and decorated ; but the most interesting ecclesiastical building is the Baptist Chapel, a spacious structure erected through the instrumentality of the Rev. William Knibb, the energetic and enthusiastic missionary who suffered much hardship and persecution on account of his labours among the slaves prior to emancipation.

Just outside Falmouth we cross the Martha Brae River, near which there is a tradition that a gold mine exists. It is said that the Spanish Governor, Don Pedro d'Esquivel, giving audience once to a cacique of the aboriginal tribes, was struck by the profusion of golden ornaments with which he had adorned his person, and demanded of him the secret of the mine. The indian refused to communicate this and was put to torture. If the secret was ever discovered, it was most effectually buried again, for no one has ever come across the mine since, and " the secret gold mine " it remains, and probably will ever remain.

Leaving Trelawny, to the East we enter the Parish of

ST. JAMES,

of which the chief town is Montego Bay, which ranks next to Kingston in point of commercial importance, as gauged by the amount of export and import duties collected. The Court House in Montego Bay is a fine building, dating from the year 1803. There is a handsome and extensive market, built some few years ago. Different religious denominations have their places of worship in the town. the most striking being the old Parish Church, which contains within its walls records of past generations of North-side celebrities, including one beautiful piece of sculpture by Chantrey. One monument in this Church has a strange story attached to it. a story which we may charitably hope to be apocryphal. This is the statue of a lady, by name Palmer, who lived at Rose Hill, an estate in the Parish of Trelawny. It is reported of this lady that she had murdered no less than five husbands, and that she herself died a violent death by strangulation. It appears strange that the memory of this female fiend should be perpetuated by a monument in church, but it is still more strange that, after the statue had been erected, there appeared round its marble neck a mark such as would be made by a hangman's rope, and that this mark had not been visible before the erection of the statue.

Montego Bay is in direct communication weekly with New York, by means of the fruit steamers of Messrs. J. E. Kerr & Co., which also carry passengers.

In the Parish of St. James there is an observatory at Kempshot in the hills, about ten miles from Montego Bay, at an elevation of 1,770 feet, which was built on his own property by Mr. Maxwell Hall, a Fellow of the Royal Astronomical Society, who now occupies the position of Resident Magistrate for the parish. Mr. Hall's scientific knowledge and the use of his observatory are at the disposal of the Government, and he has contributed many valuable additions to the meteorology of Jamaica and the West Indies generally.

The mountains among which this place lies were the scene of a long and

AT DRY HARBOUR.

bloody struggle between the Maroons and the Government during the last years of the eighteenth century. Exasperated by a gross breach of their treaty privileges on the part of the authorities, these rough mountaineers rebelled, and were eventually only subdued by the importation of bloodhounds from Cuba to hunt them down.

Ruins of fine old barracks in a delightfully healthy situation are still to be seen at Maroon Town, about fourteen miles from Montego Bay. The empty window frames and crumbling walls surrounding the level green parade-ground that once resounded to the clatter of hoofs, the clash and jingle of accoutrements and the hoarse word of command, all call up the ghastly tragedies which were enacted among the defiles of these hills, now so silent and peaceful.

A great impetus has lately been given to the commerce of Montego Bay, and its neighbourhood, by the operations of the Railway Company, which has begun an extension line which in a few month's time will connect Kingston with Montego Bay.

The Great River marks the boundary between St. James and

HANOVER,

the most westerly parish on the North-side. Crossing this on an iron bridge, the road takes us on and on through a repetition of tropical scenery, changing and rechanging at every turn, to the cliff where we suddenly come upon the land-locked harbour of Lucea, which in some respects resembles that of Port Antonio, but is of much greater size. At the end of the harbour is a bold promontory from which rise the grey walls and spire of the old church, and the square, solid buildings of the barracks with only the sky for a background, while at its extremity the battlements and embrasures of the ancient fort frown upon the waters which it once guarded. Cannon, too useless with age and rust, are still there. White sails flit across the blue water and tiny dug-outs dart to and fro. An amphi-theatre of hills frames this loveliness on three sides, on the slopes of which, green with patches of guinea grass and cane, comfortable looking houses are perched. The whole picture is eloquent of peace, of prosperity, and, above all, of health. For the livelong day the pure fresh sea-breeze sweeps across the harbour, untainted by dust, or other impurity ; and there are no malarious swamps to poison the breath of the land-wind that nightly brings refreshing coolness from the Dolphin Head, looming up yonder to the South.

The yam, which is largely cultivated in Hanover, enjoys a great reputation in the other parts of the Island and on the Isthmus of Panama.

In travelling through the interior of Hanover, especially in the immediate vicinity of Lucea, yam greets the eye at every step—that is the outward and visible sign of the yam in the shape of heavy dark green creepers growing on sticks planted in the ground. The yam itself is the root from which this creeper springs.

To the South of the Parish of Hanover is that of

WESTMORELAND.

We may reach this from Montego Bay without including Lucea in the route ; we may also go from Lucea direct, or round by way of Green Island. The first is a beautiful road leading through the finest grazing country in the Island. But for the great clumps of bamboo that constantly throw their graceful shade over the ponds and the profusion of water lilies that deck their surfaces, and remind us that we are still in the tropics, the sleek Herefords and the Shorthorns grazing contentedly on fat, clean pastures, bounded by grey stone walls, might delude us into the belief that we had suddenly been transported into some more temperate region.

There are six " pens "—as these grazing farms are called in Jamaica—in this district, namely Shettlewood, Ramble, Knockalva, Haughton Grove, Burnt Ground and Cacoon Castle, each of whose acreage runs into the thousands, and which

can show stock that would not disgrace any English Cattle show. At Shettlewood may be seen the silver-grey hides and quaint shapes of Zebu and Mysore
Cattle imported from India, whose offspring, when crossed with the native animal,
make about the most useful stock for draft purposes that can be desired.

The chief town of Westmoreland is Savanna-la-Mar, a shipping port of some
importance in the country, and does the export trade of a large number of sugar
estates on the plains in the interior, the produce of which is floated down the
Cabaritta River, one of the two navigable streams of the Island. Savanna-la-Mar
also carries on a large business in logwood, which grows abundantly there.

Savanna-la-Mar was the scene of one of the most fearful of those frequent

MONTEGO BAY.

episodes of death and disaster that occurred in the early history of Jamaica. On
the 20th of October, 1744, during a fierce hurricane, accompanied by an earthquake, which wrought havoc throughout the whole Island, a huge tidal wave
engulfed the entire town at one fell swoop, "leaving not a vestige of man, beast,
or habitation behind." A more sudden and complete catastrophe, this, than even
the destruction of Port Royal.

There is in Savanna-la-Mar an excellent school, which was endowed in the
year 1710 by Thomas Manning, who left for that purpose by his will an estate
called Burn Savannah, together with "thirteen negro slaves, one Indian slave, and
a hundred head of cattle."

Some ten miles east of Savanna-la-Mar, lies the township of Bluefields, formerly the site of the Spanish Oristan, of which, however, now no trace remains. It was

also for some time the residence of Mr. Gosse, the naturalist, and is situated on the road leading to the adjoining Parish of

ST. ELIZABETH,

which is in area the largest, and in population the second largest in the Colony. The productions and natural conditions of St. Elizabeth vary very greatly with its varied elevation. Its principal town, Black River, is a sea-port town with a fairly flourishing trade. Black River, which is built at the mouth of a river of the same name, known, however, in Spanish times as the Rio Caobana, is a neat, well-kept little place with some creditable public buildings, the most note-worthy of which are the Court House and the Episcopal Church. The river is spanned near its mouth by an iron bridge and is navigable for some miles inland, bringing down to the harbour quantities of logwood which is largely exported from the town. Good alligator shooting may be got in the Black River and fairly good fishing in some of its tributaries.

The town of Black River does not give the visitor a correct idea of the beautiful and healthy climate of the northern and central parts of this parish. The Santa Cruz Mountains bisect the parish from north to south, terminating at the southern extremity in a precipitous cliff known as the "Lover's Leap." There are several villages on these mountains and the salubrity of the climate is more than proverbial. The most popular resort is Malvern and the obliging Post Officer there will supply complete information. Dr. J. H. Clark, a medical man of some distinction, who can speak of the Santa Cruz Mountains from the experience gathered from twenty years' observation, has written a very able and appreciative article describing the salutary influences of a visit to these mountains. In reply to the question "What can I see?" put by a supposed invalid, Dr. Clark replies "There are few spots on earth where natural beauties so combine with those of man's creation to please and interest him. The beauties of nature abound on every side and to persons who sketch, or paint, there is plenty to amuse and edify; but invalids must not be encouraged to undergo fatigue or excitement in sight seeing; crowded and heated rooms, late hours, all operate injuriously and destroy entirely the beneficial influences of climate." In fact it is rather dull work having little but scenery to live on. External circumstances and conditions may produce a sensation of pleasure but happiness is of internal growth, and the visitor to, or resident in the Santa Cruz Mountains, or anywhere else, will be dull enough unless he carries within himself the sources of true happiness.

On the eastern side of these mountains the road passes through a series of large paddocks or grazing pens, ending in the precipitous hills which lead to the Parish of Manchester.

In the Santa Cruz Mountains are Schools—for boys at Potsdam, and for girls at Malvern—established by means of bequests more than a hundred years ago, by Mr. Munro and Mr. Dickenson, both of whom are commemorated by memorial tablets in Black River Church. Jamaica is peculiarly rich in educational endowments and there are few English speaking countries where a good education can be obtained at so small a cost.

Other places of interest in St. Elizabeth's parish are the Pedro Bluff where are a number of caves supposed to have formerly been Indian burying places; Mexico, where is a cave more than a mile in length, through which flows the river Black River; and Accompong, a Maroon settlement overlooking and adjoining the parishes of St. James and Trelawny.

MANCHESTER.

The Parish of Manchester is largely a mountain parish, with a healthy,

SANTA CRUZ.

bracing climate and a contented, prosperous population. Its western boundary overlooks the plains of St. Elizabeth from which it is reached by steep climbing roads. Its principal town is Mandeville, with its old-fashioned village green, flanked by the Church, Schools, Court House and general stores. The railway extension has brought Mandeville within a few hours of Kingston, the nearest railway-station being at Williamsfield. Mandeville is much resorted to by persons wishing a change of air from the heated streets of Kingston, and possesses one hotel and several boarding-houses, one of which, presided over by Miss Roy, has been immortalised by Professor Froude. The hotel at Mandeville —now known as the "Waverley," but until recently known as Brooks's Hotel— is a comfortable, well-conducted institution and can be recommended without reservation.

The scenery, in and around Mandeville, is of a less wild and romantic type than that on the north side of the Island. Undulating plains alternate with steep ascents; and tropical trees, cedars, mangoes, almonds, gum-trees, silk-cotton trees are to be seen in magnificent luxuriance. No mention of Manchester is complete without drawing attention to the oranges which grow in this parish as possibly they grow nowhere else in the world.

The only other town of any note in Manchester is Porus, a small town some ten miles from Mandeville, situated on the plains at the foot of the Manchester hills. Travelling east from Porus, either by road or by rail, the Parish of

CLARENDON

is reached. The northern and mountainous portions of this parish are populated by a prosperous negro peasantry, cultivating coffee, ginger and other vegetable products; in the southern districts are large sugar estates. The railway crosses the parish from east to west and there are three railway stations, namely those at May Pen, Four Paths and Clarendon Park. The principal town is Chapelton, a healthy place, with substantial public buildings, commanding beautiful views of the valleys through which flow the rivers Minho and Thomas. Lodging accommodation is very deficient at Chapelton, which is a matter for regret, seeing that, by reason of its easy access to and from Kingston and the undoubted salubrity of its climate, it is in every way suited to become one of the most popular health resorts in the Island. Other towns, or villages, besides Chapelton, are Rock River in the north, May Pen and Four Paths in the centre and The Alley and Milk River in the south. The most important of these small centres of population is Milk River, where is a bath the waters of which are possessed of valuable curative properties, especially for gout, rheumatism and liver complaints.

The waters of the Bath come from a small spring which flows from out the side of a hill about a hundred yards from the bank. The officially published analysis of these waters gives the following mineral constituents in 1.000 parts of water:—

Chloride of Sodium,		.			20.77
Sulphate of Soda,	-	-	e	..	3.10
Chloride of Magnesium,	-	ʋ	-	-	4.12
Chloride of Potassium,	-	.	-	-	.16
Chloride of Calcium,	-	.	-	.	1.50

with traces of lithia, bromine and silica. Unfortunately the accommodation and conveniences for the reception of guests are not proportionate to the curative qualities of the waters. In a generally healthy climate like that of Jamaica, where comparatively few people suffer from the ailments for which the Milk River Bath is a remedy, there is no chance of any large expenditure on bathing or lodging accommodation being remunerative. The charges, however, are extremely reasonable and the relief, if not the cure, is almost certain. For occupation there are fishing and rowing with now and then a shot at an alligator.

Several places in Clarendon have an interest of their own to the student of Jamaica history. At Carlisle Bay in 1694 the local militia gallantly repulsed a strong force of French invaders who had previously devastated a large tract of richly-cultivated land in what is now the Parish of St. Thomas. At Sutton's about a mile south of Chapelton, occurred in 1690 the first really formidable outbreak among the slaves in Jamaica. Morgan's Valley serves to recall the name of Sir Henry Morgan, the redoubtable buccaneer, who was Lieutenant-Governor of the Island in the latter part of the seventeenth century.

MANDEVILLE.

The last of the country parishes, taking the circuit of the Island in the order adopted in these pages, is

ST. CATHERINE.

The tourists in this parish will undoubtedly be centred in Spanish Town, founded by the Spaniards and known to them by the name St. Jago de la Vega, St. James of the Plain, so called to distinguish it from other places named after the Patron Saint of Spain. Spanish Town is between twelve and thirteen miles from Kingston, and is reached either by road or rail. From the time of the English conquest of Jamaica until 1872, this interesting little city was the capital town of the colony. In the centre of it is the Square, flanked on the side by "The King's House," built in 1762, for many years the official residence of the Governor and probably the finest building of its kind in the West Indies. Opposite the King's House is the former Legislative Hall, where for 200 years the House of Assembly held its meetings. On the north side of the square, in a handsome temple, is a magnificent statue of Rodney by Bacon, which was erected to commemorate the great victory, in 1781, of that Admiral over the French fleet under Count deGrasse, which saved the British West Indies from possible conquest; on either side of the statue are two long brass guns which were captured from the French Admiral's ship in the same battle. One of the most unpopular acts of Sir John Peter Grant, when Governor, was the removal of this statue to Kingston, when the seat of Government and most of the public offices were transferred thither from Spanish Town in 1872. This act caused a feeling of dissatisfaction for seventeen years, until in 1889, the statue was restored to its former position, under its old cupola in the Public Square of Spanish Town, amid great rejoicings. It is said that the Mango, now so common a fruit in the West Indies, is another trophy of this victory, some young trees, found in one of the French ships, having been planted in Jamaica. It is even said that some large trees growing at Berkshire Hall, not far from Linstead, are " original trees." This seems hardly likely, but it may be that they are closely descended from the trees brought by Lord Rodney.

Opposite the Temple of Rodney and forming the quadrangle with a pretty public garden in the centre are the Town Hall, the Court House and the Government Savings Bank.

The Cathedral dedicated to Saint Catherine is a building of some pretensions and by no means devoid of interest on many accounts. It is supposed to stand on the foundation of the Spanish Red Cross Church of St. Peter, which was wantonly destroyed by the English troops, on their first entry into Saint Jago de la Vega. The present building takes the place of the earlier one, built in the reign of Queen Anne, which was irreparably injured in the hurricane of 1712. Some of the monuments, tablets and slabs are older, and are extremely interesting. The church is paved with grave-stones, amongst which are those of persons who were eminent in their own times, and whose names are still remembered by posterity. Some of the grave-stones are specially interesting to Archeologists. There is one to the memory of three of a family named Assam, who had for their crest three asses engraven on the stone. Another makes it appear that an eminent man (Colbeck of St. Dorothy) died " amid great applause." A recent re-seating of the Cathedral has hidden many of these slabs, but this obscurity is compensated for by the preservation of the inscriptions, which were being obliterated by rough treatment and the tramp of feet.

The Cathedral has a beautiful east window, some fine oak carvings and several admirably executed pieces of Sculpture, the most striking of these being those erected to the memory of the Earl and Countess of Effingham, Sir Basil Kerth, Major-General Selwyn and the Countess of Elgin.

Among other places of interest in St. Catherine are the Vale of Guanaboa;

Port Henderson, with its Mineral Springs and Bath, a favourite holiday resort of
the people of Kingston and Spanish Town; on the hill at Port Henderson is
Rodney's "Lookout" from which the Admiral "watched the adjacent sea";
Apostles' Battery; Green Bay, Fort Augusta; Passage Fort, where the English
conquerors first landed; the Great Salt Pond; Old Harbour, which was a
thriving port in the days of Spanish occupation, and which, after being closed
for many years, has been reopened to the great advantage of the Island; and
Linstead, an inland town, the centre of rich and fertile districts. Between Linstead
and Spanish Town, through a lovely gorge, known as the Bog Walk, flows the Rio
Cobre. Few parts of Jamaica are more beautiful, and few will better repay a

PORUS.

visit than the Bog Walk. It has been the theme of much descriptive writing,
but there is a richness and a subtle delicacy about it which defy the power
of the pen properly to portray them.

An exceedingly comfortable and well-conducted hotel has recently been
built at Spanish Town on the banks of the Rio Cobre, from which it takes
its name. There are also private boarding-houses; living at Spanish Town is
cheap and good, the temperature is not excessively hot, whilst all the year
round the nights are cool. Spanish Town, in short, replete with historic associations and surrounded by natural charms in endless variety, quite justifies all
that has been said, or written, in its praise.

COLUMBUS AND JAMAICA.

THE main events in the life of Columbus have recently been made familiar to all readers of current literature, and will only be summarised here for the purpose of connecting Jamaica with the celebration of the fourth centenary of the discovery of the Western continent. Born in Genoa in 1436, Columbus—we use the anglicised form of his name by which he is most widely known—early embraced the life of a sailor, having previously studied at the University of Pavia "geography, cosmography, geometry, astronomy and the nautical sciences." In 1470 he married the daughter of Palestrello, a Portuguese navigator, and settled at Porto Santo, an island off the Western coast of Spain. Starting from his island home, expeditions were made from time to time to the Mediterranean and to the coast of Guinea, and were followed in 1477 by a voyage round Iceland.

Meanwhile the invention of printing by Gutenberg had given wide circulation to the ancient speculations as to the existence of a vast continent beyond the Pillars of Hercules, and to the conjectures of Greek students as to the shape of the earth. Reminiscences of the voyages and travels of Marco Polo, which were first told during his imprisonment at Genoa, together with theories about the remains of vegetable matter, unknown on the Eastern continent, which were at times washed ashore at Porto Santo, combined to arouse both the curiosity and the enthusiasm of Columbus, and to create in his mind a belief that the shores of Asia, with its fabulous stores of wealth, its ivory, its gold, its spices, could be reached by navigating to the West.

The idea once entertained was never abandoned, in spite of difficulties and opposition which would have effectually checked the ardour of many an intrepid man. There is something almost ludicrous in the picture of Columbus, going from monarch to monarch and from court to court, begging assistance to discover a new and mighty continent. His fellow-countrymen in Genoa declined the honour; King John, of Portugal, patiently listened to his plans and carefully investigated his charts and then, with a meanness which is scarcely credible, privately despatched a fleet of his own, hoping to gain for himself and his country the credit of a discovery, to the belief in the possibility of which he was Columbus's first royal convert. But the stars in their courses fought against the king; the elements, as though in disgust with treachery and dishonour, drove back the Portuguese fleet, crippled, panic-stricken and determined never again to seek the shores of India by sailing towards the setting sun. From Portugal Columbus turned to Spain, to France, to England, for help. At last, after repeated disappointments and rebuffs, the Spanish Sovereigns, Ferdinand and Isabella, espoused his cause.

and on Friday the 3d of August, 1492, at the age of fifty-six, a time of life when many men think their best work is done, Columbus sailed for the West, with a fleet of three small vessels and a crew of one hundred and twenty men.

The details of this memorable voyage are beyond the intention of these pages. But, if we are constrained to admire the persistent determination with which Columbus urged the adoption of plans which appeared to be little else than the wild dreams of a visionary, still more must we admire the indomitable energy and the constant faith which brought himself within sight of the land of promise and expectation, himself alone calm and confident, his companions on the verge of mutiny, annoyed and disgusted at being so often deceived by the false appearance of approaching land. But it was land, not indeed the Eastern extremity of an old continent, but the out-port of a new. On the 8th of October, singing birds fluttered amidst and around the sails of the ships, and the atmosphere was redolent

LUCEA.

with the odours of the shore; three days later, in the green rush of sea-weed which floated past their ships, the sailors picked up a stick, quaintly-carved and plainly the work of intelligent men, and a thorn branch covered with the red and ripe berries which seemed a proof positive that bountiful nature was making some neighbouring land bring forth her increase. On that same night Columbus, keeping lonely watch and eagerly peering through the dim darkness which was ahead of him, discerned in the distance the faint gleams of a moving light. At two o'clock on the following morning, the 12th of October, 1492, doubt and uncertainty ceased as a gun from the *Pinta* fired the welcome signal that land was in sight. Then, soon after the dawn of day, in the bright, bracing purity of a tropical morning, followed the landing, the solemn act of thanksgiving to God as Columbus and his companions knelt on the long-looked-for beach. The natives called the island on which they landed Guanihani; Columbus called it San Salvador; it is now known as Watling's Island, one of the Bahama group, in lat. 24°

N. and long. 74° W. Later on in this same voyage, Columbus sighted Cuba and Haiti, on the latter of which he left a small garrison, and then returned to Europe in triumph, taking with him Indians and curiosities and various specimens of Western produce. On the 15th of March, 1493, Columbus anchored in the harbour of Palos, from which six months before he had sailed, full of hope and confidence, though amidst the gloom and despondency of the little village, the people of which saw nothing but calamity or death in some hideous shape as the fate of their friends and relatives, who formed no inconsiderable part of the expedition. The return was the signal for royal attentions and honours, for the congratulations of the people, for boundless admiration, for unlimited adulation, for all that wealth and the world could give in tribute to hard-earned success and well-merited triumph. It is pleasing to note this bright oasis in a life of storm and toil, where ambition was for a time at ease, where success was recognised and rewarded, a life which envy, jealousy and detraction had hardly begun to blight and embitter. Those who had once been his enemies now posed as his friends, but only for a time, for he had soon to learn by sad experience, that sometimes it is wise to reflect on the truth which underlies the aphorism of the philosopher who used to say, "Look upon your friends with the thought that they may one day become your enemies."

On the 25th of September, 1493, Columbus left the Bay of Cadiz on his second voyage of discovery, and on the 3d of May, 1494, while sailing in a southerly direction from Cuba, he came in sight of "the blue summit of a vast and lofty island at a great distance, which began to arise like clouds above the horizon." Two days later—or possibly on the following day—he anchored in the harbour off the town, now known as Port Maria, on the northern coast of Jamaica. Some slight resistance was threatened by the native Indians who flocked in their canoes around the strange Spanish ship, but they were soon appeased and Columbus anchored in the harbour, which he thought the most beautiful of all he had seen and to which he gave the name of Santa Gloria, a name which can hardly be said to have survived its bestowal. Leaving his anchorage to seek more sheltered waters, Columbus put out to sea and sailed a few miles in a westerly direction to Ora Cabecca, now written Oracabessa.* The landing was not effected without opposition and protest on the part of the natives, who were treated to a shower of arrows from the Spanish cross-bows, and terrified into confused flight by a huge bloodhound, keen to scent human blood. On reaching the shore, Columbus, in the name of Ferdinand and Isabella, took formal possession of his new discovery, which he called Santiago, though it has always been known by its Indian name of Xaymaca, modernised in spelling and pronunciation into Jamaica. A few days sufficed to repair his ships and to establish friendly intercourse with the Indians, and again the voyage was continued as far as Montego Bay, called by Columbus Buentiempo (i. e. Fair Weather) Bay, because the wind was favourable for his return to Cuba. Two months later he sailed leisurely along the southern

---

* There is some discrepancy of opinion as to the exact places of anchoring and landing. Some authorities substitute St. Ann's Bay and Puerto Bueno (the modern village of Rio Bueno) for Port Maria and Oracabessa.

coast of Jamaica, receiving kindness and hospitality, but making no attempt to explore the country. At Old Harbour Bay the chief, or cacique, boarded his ship accompanied by many members of his family and staff, and, in the course of an interesting interview, proposed that he himself and all his family should return with Columbus to Spain. The offer was courteously declined, and the journey was continued till on the 19th of August, 1494, Columbus passed out of sight of Jamaica, to the south-eastern extremity of which, now known as Morant Point, he gave the name of Cape Farol.

Thus ended the first visit of Columbus to Jamaica; his second visit was paid under very different circumstances.

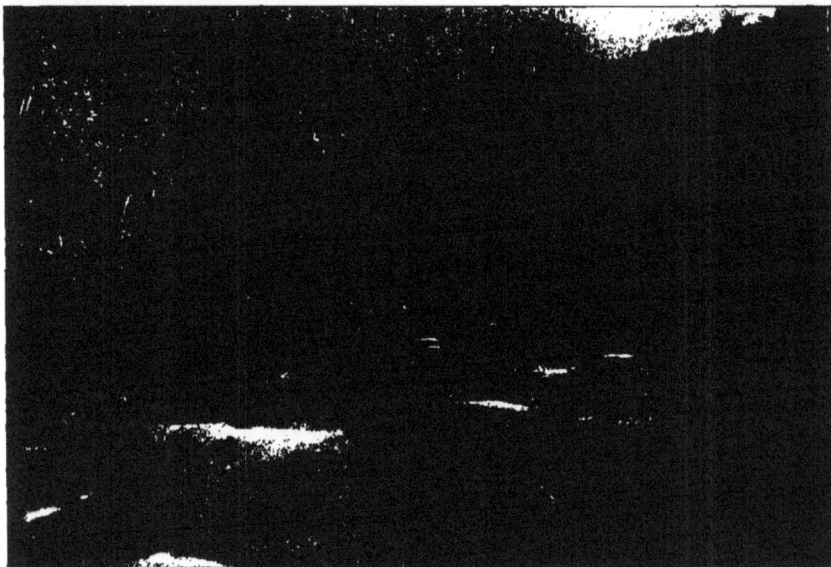

RIO COBRE RIVER.

Leaving Jamaica in 1494, Columbus did not revisit it till 1503. During the interval between these years, his position in royal and popular favour had greatly changed. In a third expedition, commenced in 1498, he had discovered Trinidad and explored the Gulf of Paria. Returning to Hispaniola (Haiti) and Cuba, he found that the Spanish settlers, to whom had fallen the original colonisation of those islands, had employed harsh measures for the enslavement of the Indians, and were quarrelling for supremacy among themselves. Columbus on the one hand protested against this action, while on the other hand his followers brought charges of incompetence and cruelty against him. Too much credence was given to these latter reports. People thought that Columbus's work for Spain was finished. It was little likely that, at upwards of sixty years of age, he would be physically capable of crossing any more unknown seas, or of setting foot on any more untrodden shores. The Spanish Court began to regret that it had showered privileges, powers, dignities, on a man of foreign, obscure origin and uncultured manners. Thus calumnies were eagerly listened to and readily believed. By Royal authority an investigation was ordered, which was entrusted to Don Francisco de Bobadilla, a self-opinionated and ambitious man. On reaching Hispaniola, Bobadilla seized on the Government, gave a free pardon to all rebels, convicts and criminals who had been imprisoned by order of Columbus and finally, without going through the form of a trial, sent Columbus and his brother back to Spain in chains.

The history of this period is almost too dramatic and exciting to bear summarising. We have the order given that the chains should be put on, the shrinking, born alike of pity and of reverence, from carrying out such an order, the final adjustment of the irons by a "graceless and shameless" criminal. "I knew the rascal," says Las Casas, "and I think his name was Espinosa." Then the return to Spain in charge of Alonzo de Villajo, an honest, kindly fellow, who did his unpleasant duty in a pleasant way. He would have struck off the irons, but his prisoner forbade him. It was under the authority of the Spanish sovereigns that the fetters were there, and by no other authority should they be removed. Home again in Spain, there occurred a re-action in his favour. His enemies had gone so far in their persecution that a strongly-felt sympathy was stirred up in his favour. The voice of the people dictated the action of the throne. Columbus was liberated and Bobadilla was dismissed and recalled, perishing in a storm at sea on his way back to Spain. Columbus, however, in spite of royal promises, was not reinstated in the privileges and dignities of which he had been deprived. Bobadilla was superseded in the government by Don Nicholas de Ovando, and Columbus, though otherwise fairly treated, had to be satisfied with a vague promise that at some not distant date, he should resume supreme command of the lands he had discovered.

But, though shelved and condemned to temporary inactivity, the mind of the great discoverer was busily at work. Vasco de Gama had rounded the Cape of Good Hope and had opened the long-wished-for route to India, so that the wealth and treasures of the East were pouring into the hands of the adventurous Portuguese. The old enthusiastic spirit was again on fire, and Columbus was full of the idea that, somewhere in the far West of the Caribbean Sea, somewhere amongst these new lands of his, he could find a strait which would be a western path to the Indian Seas.

Preparations being completed, Columbus started on his fourth and last voyage, with a fleet of four ships and crews of 150 men in all, on the 9th of May, 1502. He was then sixty-six years of age, and bore in his body traces of the toil and trouble of a hard life. But more trouble was to come, and Jamaica was to be the scene of its patient endurance. With the details of the earlier portion of the voyage we are not here concerned, and pass on to the 23d of June, 1503, when, as he himself wrote, with "his people dismayed and down-hearted, almost all his anchors lost and his vessels bored as full of holes as a honey-comb," driven by opposing winds and currents, Columbus put into Puerto Bueno (Dry Harbour). On the

following day, failing to find either sufficient food or fresh water, he sailed eastward to another harbour, since known as Don Christopher's Cove. His forlorn
and desperate condition is thus described by his greatest historian: "His ships,
reduced to mere wrecks, could no longer keep the sea, and were ready to sink
even in port. He ordered them, therefore, to be run aground within a bow-shot

IN BOG WALK, RIO COBRE RIVER.

of the shore, and fastened together, side by side. They soon filled with water to
the decks. Thatched cabins were then erected at the prow and stern for the
accommodation of the crews, and the wreck was placed in the best possible state
of defence. Thus castled in the sea, he wished to be able to repel any sudden
attack of the natives, and at the same time to keep his men from roving about
the neighbourhood and indulging in their usual excesses. No one was allowed to
go on shore without especial license, and the utmost precaution was taken to pre-

vent any offence being given to the Indians. Any exasperation of them might be fatal to the Spaniards in the present forlorn situation. A firebrand thrown into their wooden fortress might wrap it in flames and leave them defenceless amidst hostile thousands.''

Fortunately the natives turned out to be well-disposed to their visitors, and for a time there was little difficulty in obtaining, by exchange of ornaments and other trifles of European manufacture, sufficient food to support the shipwrecked crews. But the supply was not inexhaustible. The country indeed was fertile, but on the other hand, the population was large, and Columbus's men were both hungry and fastidious. Dreading the time when the supplies of the district should be exhausted and his followers reduced to famine, Columbus determined on what we may consider the first exploration of Jamaica. Diego Mendez, one of the bravest and most loyal of his officers, was sent on a foraging expedition with three other men. They travelled along the coast and a few miles inland through the present parishes of St. Ann, Trelawny, St. James and Hanover. Friendly terms were made with different chiefs—the names of two of these, Huarco and Ameyro, are preserved—and a regular supply of food was guaranteed, in exchange for fish-hooks, knives, beads, combs and such-like articles. The food to be obtained would largely consist of cassava bread, fish, birds and small animals somewhat resembling rabbits.

Mendez returned from his mission, only to be called upon for more important services. The supply of provisions was of course an immediate necessity, but the greatest need was that of means to get back to Spain, or at any rate to get into communication with Spaniards who could send ships to the rescue of the wrecked mariners. Accordingly, with a small mixed crew of Spaniards and Indians, Mendez was sent in a canoe to Hispaniola to seek assistance from Ovando and to continue his journey to Spain with despatches from Columbus. The first attempt to accomplish this hazardous undertaking was a failure. Mendez was captured by Indians and barely escaped with his life, his companions being put to death. The second attempt was successful, but many weary weeks elapsed before Columbus heard of its success. In the meantime his troubles rapidly increased. In addition to the ordinary infirmities of old age and the effects of a life of perils and exposure, he lay helplessly crippled with gout on board his stranded ship. His men lost faith in him. He had been banished, they said, from Spain. His ships had been forbidden to anchor in the harbours of Hispaniola. Mendez, it was true, had gone, but he had been sent on a secret mission to procure pardon for Columbus, who was otherwise exiled for life to Jamaica. If he were willing to attempt to escape his age and sickness incapacitated him from risking a voyage in an Indian canoe, the only available vessel of transport. They must take the matters into their own hands and at any rate secure their own personal safety. They were beyond doubt ungrateful and unreasonable, but men contemplating mutiny take little account either of gratitude or of reason. The mutiny was headed by two brothers, Francisco and Diego de Porras, the former of whom was captain of one of the caravels and the latter occupied the position of bursar and accountant-general of the expedition.

It is useless to argue with determined men. Columbus was for a moment in personal danger but his life was saved by the intervention of his brother. The mutineers were permitted to embark in ten canoes, which had been purchased from the Indians. They coasted the north of Jamaica, sailing in a westerly direction, landing here and there, pillaging, outraging, representing themselves as acting under the orders of Columbus. Two attempts to cross to Hispaniola failed and the mutineers "wandered from village to village, a dissolute and lawless gang, supporting themselves by fair means or foul, according as they met with kindness or hostility, and passing like a pestilence through the Island." To return to Columbus, the weight of his troubles was daily increasing. No news

BLACK RIVER.

came of, or from, Mendez; the supplies of provisions began gradually to decrease, until actual starvation was within easy reach. Under these circumstances it was that Columbus had resort to what has since become, in fiction if not in fact, a hackneyed and familiar trick. His knowledge of astronomy enabled him to predict that an eclipse of the moon would take place at a certain hour; this eclipse, he represented, was to be a sign that his great Deity was angry with the people for not continuing to supply him with food. The eclipse came; the Indians were amazed, alarmed, terrified. Later on, apparently in reply to the prayers of Columbus, the moon resumed her wonted functions and a plentiful supply of provisions was secured for the future.

Months passed before news came from Mendez. At last a ship anchored some distance from the shore and put off a boat. It promised badly for

Columbus when, as the boat approached his wreck, he caught sight of the ill-omened features of Diego de Escobar, whom years ago he had condemned to death, who had been pardoned by Bobadilla and partly in consequence of whose false and vindictive evidence Columbus had been displaced from his command in 1500. The ill-omen proved true ; for Escobar's relief consisted of a cask of wine, a flitch of bacon, and a letter containing vague promises of future succour. The wine and the bacon were finished long before the promises were kept. Escobar's functions, in fact, had been those of a spy, not of a friend.

Columbus took advantage of this re-opening of communications with the outer world to bring back into allegiance his rebel followers who were disheartened and worn out by the miseries and toils of a lawless and predatory life. Most of them would long before have willingly returned but they were prevented from doing so by the elder Porras. A sort of conference was held at the Indian Village of Maima—now known as Mammee Bay—a conference which ended in a free fight in which the rebels were defeated and Francisco de Porras was taken prisoner.

At last suspense was at an end, as two vessels were seen entering the harbour, one sent from Spain by the faithful Mendez, the other from Hispaniola by the treacherous Ovando, whose neglect of Columbus had so roused public feeling against him that he was driven to assume a virtue, if he had it not, and to send genuine help to the unfortunate discoverer.

Thus on the 28th of June, 1504, after a visit, which was almost an imprisonment of upwards of twelve months, Columbus left Jamaica. There is much that is pathetic about this twelve months' stay in Jamaica. It is extremely doubtful whether Columbus ever left the shelter of his stranded ships. He was an old man when he came ; toil, injustice, anxiety, disappointment had intensified the natural infirmities of old age ; gout kept him crippled in his cabin, and leaving Jamaica, he went home to die.

Coldly received by the people for the pride of whose nationality he had done so much, almost friendless, poverty-stricken, his health ruined and his spirits crushed, he lingered for two years before death mercifully set him free to embark on the last and greatest of all voyages.

> Oh strong soul, by what shore
> Tarriest thou now? For that force,
> Surely, has not been left vain!
> Somewhere, surely, afar,
> In the sounding labour-house vast
> Of being, is practised that strength
> Zealous, beneficent, firm.

Columbus died at Seville on the 20th of May, 1506, in the seventieth year of his age, not knowing, even to the last, that he was the discoverer of a new and vast continent, which was to take its name not from him but from one of his companions.

Beyond allusions and references in books and pamphlets, Jamaica contained no memorial of Columbus. Next year will see the four hundredth anniversary of its discovery, possibly the year will not be allowed to pass without something tangible being done to commemorate the person of the discoverer.

LATER HISTORY.

JAMAICA, thus discovered and acquired, remained in the possession of Spain for upwards of a century and a half. It has been said that the transactions of the Spaniards during this period, as far as Jamaica is concerned, have scarcely obtained the notice of history; to this may be added that, when the Island was added to the British possessions in the West, there were few traces that any solid and reasonable effort had been made by the first conquerors of Jamaica to utilise their opportunity for the good of the conquered province. This period is mainly memorable for the complete annihilation, often by methods pitilessly cruel and revoltingly ruthless, of the aboriginal inhabitants of Jamaica. Of these interesting people a few words may be said—interesting, because, in the imperfect records which survive their destruction, we learn little but what is good of them.

In speaking of the aboriginal inhabitants of Jamaica, it must be borne in mind that, at the time of the discovery of the West Indies, including in that term the whole of the islands lying in, or around, the Caribbean Archipelago, there were two separate races of Indians inhabiting them. One of these races, called the Caribbs, inhabited the Windward Islands and the Southern Antilles; they were a hardy, warlike people, and their descendants, having survived the influences of European civilization, still live in some islands, *e. g.* St. Vincent, Trinidad and Dominica. The inhabitants of the more Western islands, including Jamaica, were of a far gentler type; they cannot be accused of being actually deficient in courage, for they offered a certain amount of resistance to Columbus and to his successors, but their virtues were of a milder, quieter kind than those usually attributed to savage tribes. They were not cannibals; they do not seem to have been treacherous, ferocious or cruel; they were religious, with perhaps an unusually small element of superstition in their religion; they had certain quaint ideas about the Creation of the World and a tradition about a Deluge. They believed in a future state of existence, the highest happiness in which may be epitomised in familiar words as being in the possession of

"Bright maidens and unfailing vines."

They had a fixed form of Government, simple, patriarchal and dignified. They cultivated the ground just as much as was necessary for the provision of food; they had a game called *Bato*, a sort of primitive foot-ball, and they smoked tobacco, using frequently that quaint form of pipe, resembling in shape a schoolboy's wooden catapult, and consisting of one straight tube, branching off into two other tubes, which were inserted up the nostrils. They were kind to each other and hospitable to strangers, and on the whole appear to have been a harmless, simple-minded folk; perhaps, it may be said, the world would have been none the worse for the survival of this race and for the extermination of some other race less creditable to humanity.

Turning now from the original inhabitants to the first conquerors of Jamaica, the actual remains at the present day of the Spanish occupation are almost entirely confined to a few names and a few stones. The site of the first capital of the Island, Sevilla Nueva, founded by Diego Columbus, son of the discoverer, is marked only by a few stones on the estate of Seville, near St. Ann's Bay. In the town of Porus, we have perpetuated the name of the two

BRIDGE ON RIO COBRE RIVER.

brothers Porras, who headed the mutiny against Columbus. In the Pedro Plains and the Pedro River, survives the name of Don Pedro de Esquimel, one of the most brutal and cruel of the oppressors of the Indians; and many other names, both of Spanish and of Indian origin, remain, among the latter being the name Jamaica itself. The abandonment of Sevilla Nueva, for reasons which can only be conjectured, led to the settlement and building of Spanish Town, or, as it was then called, of St. Jago de la Vega; but the Spanish Town which we now know contains few traces, if any, of its original buildings. The Spaniards themselves seem to have been happy and contented. The climate was pleasant and unoppressive, the soil was rich and yielded delicious fruits in abundance; if the Spaniards in Jamaica did not make the huge fortunes acquired

by their countrymen in Cuba or Hayti, or by those who settled in the mining
districts of Mexico and South America, at any rate they were satisfied to live
a lazy, luxurious, lotus-eating existence, far away from home troubles and tur-
moils, looking on Jamaica rather as their actual, than as their adopted home.

To inquire minutely into all the causes which lead to the acquisition of
Jamaica by Great Britain, would necessitate a close review of the relations
between England and Spain during the first half century of the Stuart dynasty.
It is enough here to state that James I. and Charles I. had both given way
too tamely and too timidly to Spanish claims and pretensions, and that the
honour of England, the protection of her commerce and the safety of her subjects made it imperative on Cromwell's Government to protect British interests

MONTEGO BAY. (MOONLIGHT.)

and lives in the West Indies.   Accordingly an expedition was equipped and
armed, and left England in the Fall of 1654.   The general instructions given
to the leaders of this Expedition were "to obtain establishment in that part of
the West Indies which is possessed by the Spaniards." Admiral Penn, the
father of Penn the Pennsylvania Quaker, was in command of the fleet, and
General Venables of the land forces.   The history of this Expedition is a
record of incompetence and vacillation, of bad generalship and disgraceful man-
agement, and the only wonder seems to be that the British troops were not
ignominiously driven out of Jamaica, as they had previously been expelled from
S. Domingo.   Any sort of organised resistance on the part of the Spaniards
would have routed and annihilated the demoralised forces of the invaders. This

resistance was not forthcoming. After a miserable pretence of war, discreditable alike to victor and to vanquished, Articles of Capitulation were signed on the 11th of May, 1655. These Articles laid down that any one who wished to leave the island might do so under certain humiliating conditions, while those who remained were promised their lives and the benefit and protection of the laws of England. While considering the terms of this Treaty, the Spaniards took the opportunity of removing from the Capital as much of their property and stock as possible, so that when the British troops entered St. Jago de la Vega, they entered a deserted and half-ruined city. Then followed distress, hardships, insurbordination, famine and pestilence among the troops, while the fugitive Spaniards were attempting to re-organise themselves in the North of the Island and in mountains in the centre. Although, then, the Expedition, taken as a whole, was a signal failure, and although Penn and Venables were rightly committed to the Tower on their return home, "for having deserted the forces committed to their charge," yet Jamaica was taken and added to the British possessions. Cromwell, disappointed and disgusted at the meagre result of his efforts to break the Spanish power in the West Indies, nevertheless determined to make the best of the newly-acquired colony. Venables was succeeded by General Fortescue, who soon fell a victim to a prevailing epidemic. The troops seem to have lost heart and pluck, and, though strongly re-inforced in the following year, the British power was held by so slight a thread, that the old Spanish Governor, Don Arnoldi Sasi, felt justified in attempting to regain the island. The attempt was made and failed, for the British troops under General D'Oyley, Fortescue's successor, inflicted a severe defeat on Don Sasi's forces in October, 1658, at Rio Nueva, in St. Mary's Parish. After some months of desultory kind of guerilla warfare, Sasi and his few remaining followers managed to make their escape for Cuba from a Bay on the Northern Coast, which has since been known as Runaway Bay. Cromwell died some six weeks before the victory at Rio Nueva, and D'Oyley seems to have been left by the Home Authorities to act on his own responsibility. Richard Cromwell indeed, during his short Protectorate, declined to restore Jamaica to Spain in return for a large sum of money which was offered him, and Charles II., soon after his accession to the Throne, was proof against the plausible request that Jamaica should be given back to Spain, on the ground that it had been taken by the rebel subjects of the King of England, contrary to the treaty of peace between the two Crowns. This, however, happened in England, and the second Charles had been twelve months on the throne before he took any official notice of Jamaica. In the interim D'Oyley had not been idle: he had had a few skirmishes with the remnant of Spanish slaves who had fortified themselves in the mountain forests in the centre of the island, and who were for years (under the name of Maroons,) independent of British rule, and a constant source of trouble to successive administrations. D'Oyley had also suppressed a mutiny in the ranks of his army, caused by some of the officers and men wishing to establish a civil, instead of a military, Government, and to devote themselves to an agricultural career. This period of Jamaica history

fitly closes with the proclamation of Charles II. as King, and with the appoint-
ment of General D'Oyley as First Governor of the Colony. The documents
announcing these events were read at Caguaya, which has since, in commemoration thereof, been called Port Royal. By royal authority it was decreed that
a Council of twelve, to be nominated by the Governor, should be appointed
with power to legislate for the colony. This Council accordingly was nominated,
Courts of Justice were established, magistrates and judges were appointed,
English rule and English customs were established, although the island was not
formally ceded to the British Crown until 1670.

   The conquest, or re-conquest, of Jamaica being thus complete, its history
for many years is mainly a record of the various steps which, in spite of fre-

SPANISH TOWN CATHEDRAL.

quent interruptions and of constant dissensions, raised it to the position it held,
at the beginning of this century, of a prosperous and wealthy Agricultural
Colony. Gradually land was appropriated to soldiers who were willing to settle
down to peaceful pursuits, while numbers were induced, and in some instances
compelled by political necessities, to come from Great Britain, from Ireland
and from other West Indian Islands. A remarkably rapid change soon came
over the local industries. At the time when the English first occupied Jamaica,
the principal articles of Export consisted of Hides, and of Hog's-butter, 80,000
hogs being killed every year for the sake of their lard, which, under the name
of Hog's-butter, was sold at Carthagena. A thriving trade was done in salt,
there being large salt ponds on the Eastern parts of the Southern coast. The

Spaniards had devoted much attention to Cocoa, and almost every species of tropical fruit and vegetable grew profusely; the waters swarmed with fish, and the forests abounded in various kinds of dye-woods. In fact there seemed at the time a possibility of Jamaica being the scene of a varied and extended cultivation. In the early days, however, of this occupation it was found that both soil and climate were more adapted for the growth of sugar than those of other West India colonies, and almost every other form of cultivation had to give way to sugar. The rise and rapid growth of the sugar industry affected Jamaica socially as well materially and agriculturally; for, while English or Irish settlers could carry on agricultural pursuits in the cool, bracing, mountain districts, they were incapable of hard manual labour in the cane-growing districts in the lowlands. Hence it came to pass that the traffic in slaves and the system of slavery increased step by step with the extension of sugar cultivation. From this time dates a long period of material prosperity on the part of the owners, whether resident or non-resident, of property, and of almost equal misery on the part of the unfortunate labourers. At the same time the political Constitution of the Colony was being built up and strengthened. The Crown-nominated Council has been mentioned, and in 1664 an Assembly, consisting of thirty members elected by the people, was constituted, with power to pass laws, which, unless confirmed by the King, were only in operation for two years. This institution, notwithstanding many impediments and difficulties and in spite of constant wranglings and frequent irregularities, continued in existence for 202 years. The brighter side of the history of the Jamaica Assembly is a history of the struggle between popular rights and arbitrary power; questions of privilege were constantly turning up and were discussed and disputed with a keenness and a bitterness worthy of the English House of Commons at the present day; the relations between the Council and Assembly were often strained to the utmost limits of tension; on one occasion indeed a member of the Council seized the opportunity offered by a state dinner to kill a member of the Assembly. Governors, good, bad and indifferent, followed each other in quick succession, some such as Lord Windsor, only staying a few months, and others, like Sir Thomas Modyford, ruling for more than six years. These were rough days and there is reason to believe that Governors were not chosen out of any particular regard for their moral character and virtuous living, for we find one of them described by a contemporary as being "the most profest immoral liver in the world," and another by a friend of Pepys, who was not troubled by over-squeamishness, as being "one of the lewdest fellows of the age." Taking the early Governors as a whole it would probably be correct to say that Jamaica prospered in spite, quite as much as in consequence, of any particularly brilliant genius representing the Sovereign power. The agriculturists, as a body, the merchants, the buccaneers, rather looked on at, than participated in the game of politics. Fortunes were being made on land and on sea, and so long as money was pouring in, it mattered little to planter or merchant whether an Assembly had been illegally dismissed or a Governor been guilty of a breach of privilege.

The closing years of the seventeenth century were full of critical events in the island story. In 1689 the first, but by no means the last, destructive hurricane since the British occupation inflicted much damage on house property and growing crops, while in the following year occurred the first really serious outbreak, or rebellion, of the slaves. The number of slaves had largely increased about this time, as the first Parliament of William and Mary had opened the trade to private enterprise. Many men of rank, position and power in their native land were captured and condemned to slavery, and, naturally enough, resented the compulsory toil and the cruel treatment of the plantations. The scene of the outbreak was at Suttons, an estate about a mile from Chapelton, and it was only suppressed after considerable bloodshed and loss of property.

ROARING RIVER.

Two years later, in 1692, there happened the greatest calamity (elsewhere alluded to in these pages), which has ever befallen Jamaica, namely the earthquake in which the then-wealthy town of Port Royal was almost entirely swallowed up. This terrible catastrophe has been often described, and no fresh description can add to its horrors. The earth was shaken with such violence that on all sides were seen and heard the din and confusion caused by falling walls and buildings. Wharves, laden with valuable merchandise, private houses of wealthy men, merchants' stores together with the Church of the town and Government fortifications were all overwhelmed in one common ruin ; as the earth opened, and closed again, receiving into its bosom whole streets of houses and hundreds of terrified people, so did the sea rise in huge waves, and sweeping over the ruined and sunken town, complete the devastation. But this was not the end; for many days after, mutilated corpses floated up and down the harbour, or lay unburied on the shore, and the pestilence, which generated from these putrefying corpses, claimed almost as many victims as had the earthquake shocks. Nor was the destruction confined to Port Royal, for nearly every district in the Island suffered, some more seriously than others, but all to an extent which seems incredible. One familiar, and we believe fully-substantiated, case of extraordinary escape must not be omitted from any record of this dreadful visitation. At Green Bay, on the opposite shore to Port Royal, is the tomb of Lewis Galdy who died in 1739. The inscription on the tomb records that Galdy was swallowed down by one earthquake shock, and that, before life was extinct, a second shock cast him up again into the sea, whence he escaped by swimming to a boat. He lived for nearly a half a century after this adventure, was a member of Assembly and a respected merchant in Port Royal.

PORT ROYAL FROM CLOCK TOWER.

In the century succeeding the earthquake there is a wonderful sameness, though by no means a monotony or an absence of excitement, in the history of Jamaica. The political and legislative record is one of constant squabbling, impeachments, breaches of privilege and abrupt dismissals of Assemblies. The placidity and repose of tropical life were in turn and often disturbed by hurricane, earthquake, fire, pestilence and famine. There were military and naval troubles with the French and the Spaniards, the most notable perhaps being in 1702, when Benbow lost his life, and in 1784 when Rodney, by a brilliant victory over De Grasse, scattered the Fleet containing the French troops intended for the invasion of Jamaica. The Maroons, still unconquered, carried on their guerilla warfare and plundered the settlers' plantations, there were numerous insurrections, some more formidable than others, of slaves in various parishes of

the island, while the exciting life of the pirate, or privateer, increased the
wealth of Kingston and of Port Royal. Existence, amid the stirring scenes and
thrilling incidents of this sort, could surely be neither dull nor uneventful. The
space, however, at our disposal compels us to hurry over this period thus briefly,
and to pass on to the great event which influenced Jamaica more even than
war, hurricane or legislative squabbling could do; we refer to the Agitation

ROADWAY, CANE RIVER.

which culminated in the Abolition of the vile system of slavery. It is impossible to fix the exact date when this struggle commenced, for, during the
earliest days when the traffic in human flesh was recognised as legal, there were
not wanting men in England, and elsewhere, who were found to protest against
it. The day is happily past when it is necessary to denounce so hideous a
traffic, and happily, too, bitter feelings, inherited from a bitter past, are rapidly

dying away. A few figures will show the magnitude of this Trade, as far as Jamaica is concerned. Between the years 1700 and 1786 no less than 610,000 slaves were landed in Jamaica, of whom 160,000 were re-exported to other parts of the West Indies or to America. Thus more than 5,000 were added every year to the existing number. The reason for this large and constant increase may partly be that the amount of land under cultivation was being greatly extended, but it was certainly partly due to the hard labour and harsh treatment which retarded the natural increase of the population and to the fact that the number of male slaves imported was much in excess of the number of female. Added to this must not be forgotten the heavy mortality among the slave population on the not infrequent occasions of famine, pestilence or hurricane. That the treatment was cruel goes without saying. A cruel system can only be worked by cruel means and enforced by cruel laws, and the ridiculous fallacies by which its upholders endeavoured to defend it may fitly be taken as illustrations of the depth of absurdity and of groundless, or false, statements to which the champions of a wicked cause are bound to be driven in fighting against truth and light.

Perhaps the first definite step in the direction of Emancipation was a decision, in the reign of William and Mary, of the Chief Justice (Holt) of England to the effect that " one may not be a slave in England." However, this and similar decisions failed to arouse Englishmen to a sense of the iniquities which were being prepetrated under the protection of the British Flag. In 1765, Granville Sharpe was led to take up the subject, and in 1772, by his efforts, he gained the judicial decision that " as soon as any slave sets his foot on English ground he is free." One cannot help wondering how this decision did not at once, and permanently, settle the question, for it seems natural to draw the conclusion that if the possession of slaves was wrong and illegal in England, it was theoretically equally wrong and illegal in other parts of the British Empire, that, if the putting the foot on British soil in Kent or Devonshire could bestow freedom, the same privilege belonged to British soil in Jamaica or Trinidad. But the day of Justice was still far distant. Reports of cruelty and of revolting ill-treatment roused indeed the heart of philanthropic England, but the West Indian interest was in those days, politically, commercially and socially, far more powerful than any sentiment however philanthrophic, or any sense of justice however deeply-rooted. Other causes too combined to impede the progress of the agitation. The French Revolution, with its indirect, but terrible, consequences in Hayti, was not the least among these, while Royal influence was not wanting against the cause of Right, the Duke of Clarence, afterwards William IV., having been in Jamaica, and retaining a strong feeling of regard for the slave-holders. Resolutions were moved from time to time in both Houses of Parliament, but only to be lost, although the number of adherents to the cause was daily increasing in the country. At length in 1807 a measure was passed abolishing the Trade in slaves from the 1st of March, 1808. This measure, while preventing further importations, did not affect the condition of the existing slaves. Meanwhile the Jamaica Legislature had seen the necessity of action of some sort, and several

Acts were passed with the professed object of ameliorating and modifying the conditions of slavery. The first important step, after the suppression of the Trade, was the compulsory Registration of slaves, the intention of which was to make it impossible to secretly revive the slave Trade by clandestine importations. Amid much opposition and a good deal of undignified protest on the part of the Assembly, this Act was passed, care being taken on the part of the Government to assure the Assembly that the measure was not meant to be a step towards Emancipation. Whether intended or not, it was such a step. Although the actual Emancipation was opposed point by point, and step by step, by the planting body in Jamaica and in England, yet every one knew that it was merely a matter of time, the length or shortness of which depended

RODNEY MONUMENT, SPANISH TOWN.

entirely on circumstances. Some of these circumstances have been referred to above; they might be strong enough to delay, but were powerless to prevent, for when the Trade was suppressed, the System was doomed.

In 1823 Canning got the House of Commons to pass Resolutions recommending such reforms in the Code as might prepare the slaves for a participation in those civil rights and privileges which were enjoyed by other classes of His Majesty's subjects. These Resolutions having been passed, the West Indian Governors were directed to carry their provisions into effect. This the Jamaica Assembly refused to do, representing that the Slave Code was complete, and that the slave population was as happy and comfortable as the labouring classes in any part of the world. In other slave-holding colonies the Resolutions of the House of Commons were loyally carried out and, in all likelihood, it was the obstinate and perverse resistance of the Jamaica Assembly which hastened the day of Freedom. Allowance must perhaps be made for the conduct of gentlemen whose interests were, in their own judgment, wrapped up in the continuance of slavery, and who foresaw in Emancipation nothing but Ruin and Disaster both to themselves and to the colony at large, but it must be conceded that an Assembly, so constituted, was utterly unfit to decide impartially a question in which they were personally so deeply interested. Naturally enough fresh rebellions broke out among the slaves, who had gathered from conversation, overheard and repeated, that Emancipation had been agreed on in England, but was being withheld in Jamaica. In one of these rebellions about this time, property to the value of £666,977 was destroyed, and the proprietors were so impoverished, that the Home Government had to grant a loan of £200,000 to replenish the devastated plantations. It is to be noted that almost all risings of slaves were characterised by the burning of crops and of planters' houses, fire being almost the only weapon within reach of the insurgents. The wrath of the owners was then poured out on the teachers of religion. The violence of the language used and the unfounded nature of the charges alleged against missionaries may well be regarded as signs of the consciousness of the weakness of the cause. To assert that "ample provision had been made for the proper instruction of slaves" was as untrue as it was a ridiculous piece of bounce for the Assembly to "threaten the transfer of their allegiance to the United States, or even to assert their independence after the manner of their continental neighbours." Again we are compelled by want of space to abstain from details—details in some cases as disgusting as they are disgraceful.

We hasten to the end of the struggle. In 1832 the Earl of Mulgrave arrived and entered on his memorable Governorship. He at once insisted on Canning's Resolutions of 1823 being embodied in the Island legislation. The infatuated Assembly again asserted its independence of the British Parliament. To allow the House of Commons to legislate was "subversive of the common rights and dangerous to the lives and liberties of the colonists." The Assembly acknowledged indeed the Supremacy of the Crown, but refused to "admit the supremacy of a portion of His Majesty's subjects in the Parent State over another portion of these subjects in Jamaica." After this, all other efforts having failed, the Imperial Parliament had no alternative but to pass the Emancipation Act. This was in May, 1833, when it was enacted that on and after the 1st of August, 1834, all slaves should be free, this freedom to take effect after an intermediate period of apprenticeship of six years for predials, or field labourers, and of four years for domestic servants. The Government proposal to advance a loan of £15,000,000 was altered into a grant of £20,000,000, as compensation to the slave-holders. In October of the same year, the Island Assembly met to consider the Imperial Act, which was ungraciously accepted. The old blustering independence was by no means dead, but had to content itself with an impertinent declaration that the action of the Imperial Parliament was unconstitutional, and involved a policy of "spoliation which could produce nothing but discontent and rebellion." Thus on the 1st of August, 1834, slavery ceased and the apprenticeship system commenced. Pecuniary compensation, amounting to £5,853,975, was paid to Jamaica owners in consideration of the manumission of 255,290 slaves, while 55,780 slaves, consisting of children, old people and runaways, were excluded from the compensation. The apprenticeship system was not allowed to run its allotted time, for in

THE ALTAR, PARISH CHURCH, KINGSTON.

June, 1838, following, the Legislature in the mother country, though strongly protesting against the interference of the Imperial Parliament, it was decided by the Jamaica House of Assembly to close the apprenticeship on the 1st of August in that year. Accordingly, on the 1st of August, 1838, absolute and unconditional freedom was granted to the slave, or apprentice, population of Jamaica.

It is not our intention here to narrate the further history of the Colony, but we cannot close without a slight review of the progress and development of the emancipated negroes. There have been those who have asserted that there is in the African race an ethnological inferiority which makes it unreceptive of the highest civilisation. This opinion, however, is necessarily an *a priori* begging of the question and by no means leads logically to the *a posteriori* conclusion that all attempts at civilisation have failed, are failing and must fail. Not the most sanguine friend of the negro ever expected that his complete civilisation would be effected in a day, or even in a century. Favourable surroundings and sufficient time have been, and are, always and everywhere, essential conditions for the growth of the higher civilisation, and those who know the African race best do not doubt for a moment what the result will be when these conditions have been fully realised. We venture to say that there is no half-century in the whole history of civilisation, in which greater advancement has been made by any race than has been made by the West Indian British negroes in the half-century which elapsed in August, 1888, since the complete emancipation of their race. Like other human beings, they have their faults, many and great, but, in the majority of cases, they are the faults of a child rather than the vices of a man ; their virtues, too, may be the virtues of a child, docility, affection, simplicity, but who will say that these cannot grow into the virtues of a man? Whether ethnologically inferior or not, they started fifty years ago, heavily handicapped with the vices which had come down to them from the days of the African heathenism of their race, or which were incidental to their condition as slaves. They started without money, with little or no education, with violent prejudice against them, to compete in the battle of life with their former owners, men of means, men of education and influence, men holding the reins of government. Now, after the lapse of half a century, we find them exercising political power in an intelligent and contented spirit ; among their number are lawyers, doctors, clergymen and schoolmasters, talented, successful and respected members of their professions ; there are a few wealthy planters and merchants, and there is a large body of small peasant proprietors—without its parallel outside the West Indies—an industrious, honest and God-fearing set of men, acquiring and practising year by year those habits of steady application, intelligence and self-reliance, which are as essential to the black man's success as they are to that of the white. If we were asked to point to the results of Emancipation in Jamaica, we would do so by means of a contrast. Little more than fifty years ago there were more than 300,000 persons of African descent in Jamaica, held in unnatural bondage by alien tyrants, perpetually driven by cruelty and hardship to rebellion, which was futile in all save in increasing the cruelty, deprived of the rights of citizenship and often of the privileges of humanity, existing the existence of cattle rather than living the lives of men and women. Look on that picture and now look on this. There are in Jamaica at the present time upwards of half a million persons, African by descent, but British subjects by birth, speaking the English language, enjoying English institutions, with an English literature and English laws, loyally bound by ties both of gratitude and of expediency to the English Throne.

SPORT IN JAMAICA.

THERE are other amusements for the tourist in Jamaica than the feasting of the eye on beautiful scenery. This being a British Colony, first and foremost comes naturally the national British game of Cricket.

There are several cricket clubs in Kingston and about the Island, but chief among them all stands, as it ought to, the Kingston Cricket Club, with a total membership of about 300. The Club owns a first-class ground at Sabina Park, on the outskirts of Kingston, and numbers among its members all the foremost cricketers of the Island. It is constantly being recruited by new blood in the shape of officers of the Garrison, fresh from English schools and colleges, and so can always put a formidable eleven into the field. Indeed Sabina Park is classic ground for Americans; for there in January, 1888, the team of American cricketers who were making a tour of the West Indies were defeated by the picked strength of the Kingston Club. This reverse, however, they atoned for, by beating in succession the St. Elizabeth, the Garrison and the Portland Clubs.

Besides the cricket ground the Club possesses on the same place three excellent lawn tennis courts, where play is permitted every day of the week, Saturday excepted.

Friends introduced by members of the Club are cordially welcomed.

Jamaica, by the way, contributed seven men to the team of cricketers, from the West Indies, who visited the United States and Canada in 1886; where, out of thirteen matches played, they won six and lost five, while two were left drawn.

The premises of the Royal Jamaica Yacht Club are pleasantly situated at Rae Town, a suburb of Kingston. Cool, airy rooms are these, close to the beach, with the pure sea-breeze blowing through them all day. Billiards and whist are provided for and there is a reading room supplied with the latest magazines and papers. Several of the members own small yachts, and on every important public holiday a regatta is held, that on the Queen's Birthday, the 24th of May, being the chief. One also takes place during the visit of the North American and West Indian Squadron of the British Fleet about the month of April.

On all these occasions, among the events are races for fishing canoes, pulling and sailing; and most picturesque is the sight of these frail hollow logs—for they are nothing else—tearing along through the waves, if there be a strong breeze, with the leech of the one sail trailing in the water half the time, and the half-naked crew sitting up on the weather gunwale busily baling out the water that is shipped by the bucketful.

Jamaicans do not yield to the inhabitants of any country in their enthusiasm for the sport of racing.

Every year about a fortnight before Christmas a meeting is held in Kingston, which lasts three days, and comprises fourteen or fifteen events. The principal prize is the Queen's Purse, which is regulated by a law of the Island, passed by a sporting legislature of the old days, but owing to the impetus lately given to this pastime by a few energetic young sportsmen, other purses outstrip it in value.

But although that is the case, the winner of the Queen's Purse, a three-mile race, is generally regarded as having carried off the "blue riband" of the

CROSSING A RIVER.

Jamaica turf. At this meeting compete descendants of some of the best blood to be found in the English Stud Book, and the race of thoroughbreds is preserved from degeneracy by the constant importation of mares and stallions from England, for each of which the Government awards a bounty.

Those interested in turf matters may derive the most complete information by consulting the Jamaica Stud Book recently compiled by Mr. J. T. Palache. of Manchester.

Race meetings are also held at Cumberland Pen, a quarter of an hour from Kingston by rail, and at Black River.

St. Elizabeth, Manchester and St. Ann's are the parishes in which racers are principally bred.

The Kingston race-course is a breezy stretch of common to the north of the city, commanding a fine view of the Palisadoes and the harbour to the south, and looking up northwards to the dim and distant Blue Mountain Peaks, the white huts of Newcastle perched on one of the ridges in bold relief, and the encircling sweep of the foothills embracing the Liguanea Plain, while the dark blue barrier of the Long Mountain bounds the view eastward.   It is a noble setting, and one that cannot be surpassed by any other race-course in the world.

The track is oval in shape and just one mile in length.   On the western side is an iron grand stand, underneath which are bar rooms, weighing rooms and other offices, with a railed enclosure in front.   Flanking this, a strip of garden north and south divides the course from the road.

A NATIVE FISHING BOAT.

Although we have no large game in Jamaica there is plenty of shooting for the sportsman who is content with wild-fowl.

Of game birds we have the blue pigeon, the baldpate, the whitewing, the peadove, the whitebelly, the partridge and, last and most delicious of all, the ringtail.

Of these all, with the exception of the whitebelly, partridge and ringtail, may be shot from the 26th of July to the last day in February, the open season for the three just mentioned dating from the first of September.   A gun license costs eight shillings.

The blue pigeon and the baldpate are strong-winged sporting birds that take a good deal of shooting when in a hurry.   The whitewing is a smaller pigeon and flies more in flocks than the others.   The peadove is generally to be found singly or in pairs along the roads or on commons, or in dry river courses, and he will carry away more shot for his size than any other bird. The whitebelly and the partridge never fly in the open. They haunt thickets in the woodland where the underwood is not too dense. The ringtail is a denizen of the high mountains and shooting him is very toilsome work.

In addition to these, we are visited every winter by large flocks of duck and teal, escaping from the rigours of the North American climate.

The best time for shooting is in the grey dawn of the morning, and for a couple of hours after sunrise, for then the birds leave the roost and fly off to the feeding grounds in the case of pigeons, and the ducks and teal come out of the sedges and disport themselves in the open spaces on the ponds and marshes.

SPANISH TOWN RIVER.

Exceedingly pleasant are these morning excursions when, starting from your home before daylight, you watch the grey morning light flicker up, and see the first red streak of the coming sun set aglow the eastern sky, and breathe the dewy freshness that everything exhales in this, the sweetest hour of the whole day's round. And when you have got into position, how your nerves tingle at the cry of "mark" as a plump baldpate comes whizzing along overhead; and how satisfying the crack of the gun and the thud that follows it, as your first bird falls headlong, a crumpled heap of feathers!

Most exciting of all is the alligator hunt. It is difficult for any but the practised eye to detect the small portion of his snout and the caverns that conceal his eyes, which are all that the beast shows above the surface of the water as he paddles warily along; and it is almost as difficult to distinguish him from a log of wood as he lies basking in the sun at noonday, with his tail and hind paws in the shallow water and his head and the forepart of the body recumbent on the margin of the lagoon or the bank of the river.

A Winchester rifle is a very handy weapon for the slaughter of this beast, and his most vulnerable points are the skull just in the region of the eyes, and the body immediately behind the forepaws. But the shot must in either case be fair and true.

This sport, however, should only be undertaken by those who can stand exposure to the burning rays of a mid-day sun, and who are proof against the noxious exhalations of malarious swamps ; so we will advise the stranger, if in search of health, to leave it alone.

The Blue Mountain forests teem with wild hogs, but the hunting of these is a vocation which demands a special training. The professional hog hunters

ON THE NORTH COAST ROAD.

are a race of men who are built of nothing but bone and sinew, past fattening by any process of diet. They go out armed with muzzle-loading fowling pieces of antique and precarious structure, which they charge with a liberal allowance of bits of lead and old nails. They are accompanied by a couple or two of lean mongrel dogs, contemptible to look at, but of marvellous endurance and agility. After camping out for a night, they start early on the following morning, and are pretty certain soon to come across fresh hog "sign," as they term it. The dogs begin to sniff the air and whimper, and after circling round for a minute or two with noses to the ground, dash off in one direction followed by the hunter, as they go crashing through the underwood, crossing precipitous gorges and splashing through the crystal streams that rush down them, hurling themselves down steep mountain sides at an angle of forty-five degrees, and toiling up an equally abrupt ascent with scarcely diminished speed, every foot of it covered with dense forest. Presently they give tongue, and the hunter knows that the quarry is sighted, and soon an angry grunting tells him that it is brought to bay. Then he yells out encouragement to his dogs, calling each by name, and struggling and crashing through the forest draws near enough to give the gallant boar his *coup de grace*. Often the dogs get the worst of it ; and the writer of this once joined in a hunt which, although five dogs were engaged, resulted in a loss of the game and the death of one dog, while another was so sorely injured that his wounds had to be stitched up.

A boar standing two feet six inches at the shoulder is by no means a rarity; and the writer has seen, far in the recesses of the Blue Mountain forests, fresh tusk marks on trees and saplings at a height of three feet six inches from the ground.

Wherever the hog is killed there the camp is pitched—water is always near by in these wonderful mountains—and, a fire being kindled, the process of "jerking" is begun. That is a slow grilling over a wood fire, among the embers of which aromatic leaves are cast, while powdered pimento seed and salt are sprinkled upon the meat. The dogs are amply rewarded by the offal, and soon curl themselves, gorged, as near the fire as they can creep, to enjoy a well earned rest. Night comes down, the strong land-breeze rushes seaward from the Peaks singing a mournful dirge among the treetops ; the fitful glare of the fire throws weird shadows among the tall trees, eclipsing the twinkle of the firefly that flits among the leaves ; and all is silence and slumber, save when a gaunt figure steals out of the hut, its lean proportions doubly grotesque in the uncertain firelight, to watch the progress of the grilling of the prized meat.

If their luck is good they may take three or four hogs in a couple of days, as much as they can carry home ; and the meat prepared as above described is readily disposed of at ninepence and sometimes a shilling a pound ; for when properly done it is a most toothsome morsel, and perfectly clean and wholesome, as the food of these wild hogs consists entirely of roots, berries and fruit, and their drink of the purest water.

Any more health-giving amusement than a few days of hog hunting among the Blue Mountain forests it is almost impossible to conceive ; but, as already intimated, one must be in first-rate condition.

Votaries of the "gentle art" may also find recreation in the land of the forest and the stream. And it would indeed be strange if no fish were to be found in those waters, from the very abundance of which our Island derives its name.

In the lower reaches of the rivers near the coast, especially where the waters form tidal basins, and are impregnated by the sea, some of the most delicious fish are to be found ; chief among them the callipeva and the snook. There is also a description of mullet that swims in shoals, and is generally taken with a cast net.

Higher up, in the pools below the white rush of the rapids and the leap
of the waterfall among the ferns, our celebrated mountain mullet are to be
found.   Eels and mudfish are also common in all the streams, as well as crayfish
and prawns.

But all of these are exceedingly practical creatures, and owing no doubt to
the lack of brilliant-hued winged insect life which skims across the surface of the

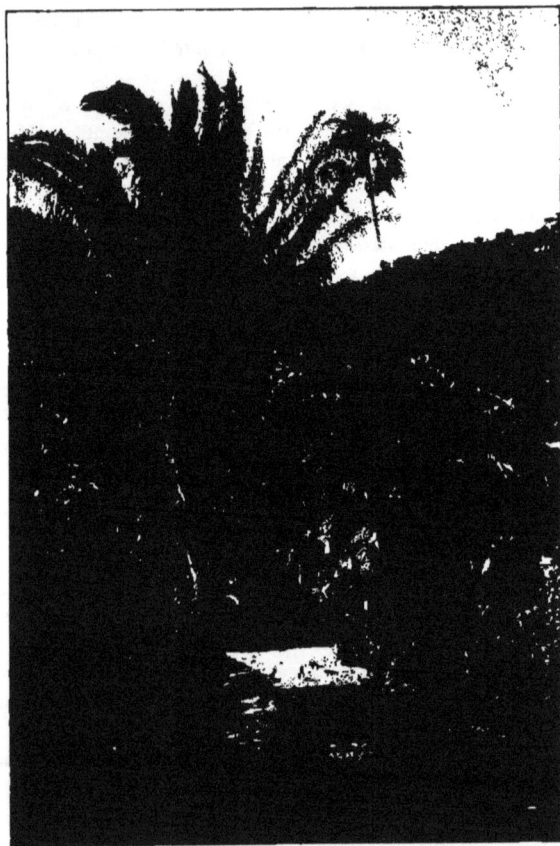

PALMS IN CASTLETON GARDENS.

water and forms the food of the fish in more northern regions, they, as a rule,
decline to be tempted by any fly, however gaudy.   Some of our local enthusiasts
in the art of angling do however succeed in making them take specially prepared
ones ; but they are easily caught by such bait as Avocado pear, and the berries of
the sweetwood and other trees.

The mudfish, eels and crayfish, are caught in bamboo basket-work " pots " laid at the bottom of the pools, and baited with something good to eat.   A piece of cocoanut meat roasted is a never failing allurement.

There are miles upon miles of crystal rivers among the gorges of the Blue Mountains into which no hook has ever been cast.

Legislation has of late years been found necessary to preserve the river fish from the indiscriminate destruction wrought by the negro methods of catching them.   Chief among these was the construction of a dam across some tolerably swift and shallow rapid, into which at intervals funnel-shaped pots were fixed. Into these, fish of all sizes were swept by the force of the current, and instantly killed, being often terribly mangled.   These weirs are now illegal, and the fish have been further protected from sportsmen of all sorts and conditions by the establishment of a close season.

PARK LODGE.

After having been directed to spawn " by Act of Parliament " at three different seasons of the year, the period between the 30th of June and the 1st of October has now been decreed as that during which they shall multiply and increase, unmolested by rod or net or fish-pot.

In concluding this chapter we would say that in attempting any of the different varieties of sport which we have touched upon, it will be necessary to form acquaintance with some resident of the country who will be able to put you "up to the ropes."

But that, as we have already said, will not prove a difficult matter in a land where every decent stranger is taken by the hand and treated as a friend till he proves himself the reverse.

THE BLUE MOUNTAINS OF JAMAICA.

THE first object that greets the eye of the voyager as he nears the shores of this Island is the mass of dark blue mountain looming up on the horizon; and as he draws nearer and nearer, though clearer and more distinct the shapes that peak and ridge may assume, each still retains the tint of deep, deep azure that gives its name to the range.

From its highest point, 7,500 feet above the sea, it throws out branches north and south, which now open out into alluvial plain, now descend sheer into the girdle of paler blue sea that encircles the Island.

And from that highest point down to where the foam of the breakers curls around its feet, it is majestic, beautiful, fraught with a thousand legends of bygone times, and clothed with a thousand different forms of vegetable life in the dark woods that re-echo the roar of the streams thundering down each gorge.

Up on those towering peaks whose heads daily wreathe themselves in a white robe of fleecy mist, or don the leaden crown of the thunder-cloud, under the yacca and the soapwood is the lair of the wild hog; and among the branches resounds the mournful "lookoo" of the ringtail pigeon, the scream of the parrot and the plaintive note of the solitaire. These with the sough of the wind among the tree tops and the roar of the torrent in the ravines make nature's concert.

Whole forests of graceful tree-ferns are there; orchids garnish the gnarled limbs that do eternal battle with the wind; mosses, green and gold and gray, clasp the knotted trunks or float pendant in the air. Strange fungi of brilliant hues crops out of the ground, where the foot of the hunter falls noiseless on the carpet of dead leaves centuries deep.

Fairy forms of fern overarch the crystal stream and kiss its frothing surface with their trailing fronds. Brilliant blossoms nod aloft on the mighty trees and blush among the thickets.

And among all this we may wander for weeks together in silent commune with nature, with no chance of seeing a human form, and no fear of encountering a dangerous or noxious wild beast or reptile.

The naturalist will find abundance of new material in the shape of ferns, orchids, flowers and fungi; the lover of the woods for their own sake will be able to gratify his passion to the full; and the practical man in search of land to cultivate will surely say: "What magnificent soil!"

The most striking Peak of the Blue Mountains in approaching Jamaica from the eastward is the Sugar-loaf, which rises sharp, distinct and isolated, about forty miles, as the crow flies, from the eastern extremity of the Island. Although eminently fitted by its shape and situation to be the highest point of the range, by some mistake, it is not, that distinction being enjoyed by the most westerly of a cluster of three "humps" rather than Peaks, which are connected with the Sugar-loaf by a precipitous ridge of about a mile and a half in length. This ridge is in parts so narrow that it is literally possible to sit astride of it; and were it not for the profuse vegetation that covers its sides, it would be indeed giddy work to look down them.

From here westward the main ridge runs along the centre of the Island, dividing the Parishes of St. Andrew and St. Mary, and it may be said to

CASTLETON GARDENS.

terminate at Stony Hill, ten miles to the north of Kingston. None of the other points approach the highest within 2,000 feet, with the exception of Sir John's Peak on the Government Cinchona Plantation, which is 6,100 feet high. This, however, is on an off-shoot trending southwards, and not on the main ridge proper.

These southern and western slopes are largely cultivated and inhabited. Here are situated all the principal coffee plantations of this part of the Island. Turning east and north we behold only virgin forest, the home of the ringtail and the wild hog, rarely trodden by human foot.

And on both sides shoot out great spurs, which in their turn send forth other spurs, which again branch out into numberless ridges, all intersected by ravines, so that the aptness of the description of the great Columbus, when he likened Jamaica to a crumpled sheet of paper, at once becomes obvious.

In the hollows of these manifold ridges lie valleys of the richest vegetable soil that one can conceive, virgin land, absolutely untouched by cultivation. Down each gorge rushes a stream of a purity that puts the very crystal to shame, wasting day after day tons upon tons of potential water power.

Coffee, the natural product of these mountains, grows here to perfection, and bears in almost incredibly short time. As an instance of this we may be allowed to quote the case of some two hundred acres of virgin soil recently planted in coffee by Captain G. G. Taylor, of Moy Hall, a retired

MONTEGO BAY FROM CHURCH TOWER.

English officer, who settled in these mountains. Having the necessary capital he proceeded to clear and cultivate at an elevation of from 4,000 to 5,000 feet, in the Parish of St. Thomas, on the southern slope of the Peak. In two years some of the coffee actually began to bear; in four it was all in bearing; and now the crops are coming in upon him so thick and fast that he was for a time seriously put about for the necessary space for curing and storing. He has now commenced clearing some one hundred and fifty acres more. When that shall have been completed and planted Moy Hall will be the most extensive coffee plantation in Jamaica, and a perfect mine of wealth to the fortunate owner.

And when we remember that the climate of these mountains is such that Europeans can labour in the open air without discomfort, and English flowers, fruit and vegetables grow easily, it will be seen that here is an El Dorado indeed. The principal difficulty is of course the means of transport and locomotion, for owing to the mountainous character of the country everything has to be done on horse or mule-back.

On the northside of the eastern end of the Blue Mountain range, in the Parish of Portland, on the lovely Cuna Cuna Pass to which allusion has already been made, lies the Maroon settlement of Moore Town. Every ridge of this portion of the range is alive with legends of the Maroon wars; for here was the principal haunt of those bandits of the old, dark days; and here, far back in an almost inaccessible fastness of rocky mountain precipice was their stronghold of Nanny Town.

About the year 1730, "The Maroons had grown so formidable under a "very able leader named Cudjoe that it became necessary to increase the "military strength of the Colony and to erect extra barracks. Every barrack "was provided with a pack of dogs by the Church wardens of the parish to "guard against surprises at night and for tracking the enemy in the mountain "fastnesses." Nanny was one of the wives of this same Cudjoe, and her name is a household word among the Maroons to the present day. She appears to have had the reputation of being possessed of supernatural power, and many remarkable feats are still ascribed to her.

Chief among them was the pot which she kept boiling at the junction of the two rivers, just below the site of Nanny Town, without any fire underneath, into which the soldiers and militia who were operating against the Maroons fell and perished when they looked into it. The whole region about Nanny Town teems with legend; and the belief in the weird stories is not confined to negroes alone, as we shall presently show. After defying for years all attempts to dislodge them, the Maroons at length succumbed in 1734 to the intrepidity and skill of a Captain Stoddart, who cut a path through the forest and dragged up two small mountain howitzers. Bringing these to bear upon the settlement he created such a panic among the Maroons, who had probably never seen or heard of cannon before, that most of those who were not actually killed by the discharge hurled themselves over the precipices and were dashed to pieces among the adamant rocks below. To quote the words of a recent historian: "The spot is now and has been ever since a scene of "superstitious awe to the Maroons; it is difficult if not impossible to per- "suade one to guide the traveller to the place. The spirits of those slain in the "battle are said to linger there; while it is a fact that men whose personal "courage is unquestionable have been bewildered by the strange mysterious noises "they hear when camping down for a night. The fears of the Maroons have "affected their own spirits, for the falling stones are no doubt occasioned by the "wild hogs rooting among the hills; and the flapping of the wings of strange "low-flying creatures is occasioned by sea-going birds who roost among these mighty "heights and before dawn hasten away to the ocean below."

And in truth it is a spot worthy to be the scene of ghost stories. Far away from everywhere, in the heart of the Blue Mountain range, the Main

Ridge throws out two large spurs that trend northward, and that in their turn, as above described, again shoot out cross ridges. Two of these converge at a height of 3,700 feet and fall in almost a sheer precipice of adamant rock 900 feet high into a river that roars along in the narrow gorge at their feet. The river is formed by the junction of two others that gush out from behind the ridges, and where they meet the eternal beat of the plunging waterfall has hollowed out a cauldron in the iron rock, which it keeps full of seething, but ice-cold water. Here you have the mysterious "Nanny's Pot." This spot can scarcely be surpassed on the face of the earth for wild and romantic beauty. On one hand the Stony River, the principal stream, which flows along

GARDENS, SPANISH TOWN.

the site of the old stronghold 900 feet above, descends this abyss in three leaps, the last of which is over a perfectly perpendicular wall of rock 150 feet high. Over this it flows in a silvery cascade that throws broadcast into the air a myriad sparkling gems, and forms tiny rainbows wherever its course is broken by a slight inequality in the face of the rocky wall. On the other hand the waters of the Nanny River come tearing down into Nanny's Pot, keeping the ferns and grasses that fringe its sides and nestle in every crevice in a prepetual state of agitation by the displacement of the air. On every side tower black rocks with surfaces polished by the flow of centuries, glistens and sparkles water of crystal purity, and nod and gleam and nestle green and gold mosses, ferns and lichens bejewelled by irridescent dew-drops, all shaded by tall forest trees between whose leaves the sun casts mottled shadows on the loveliness beneath.

A paradise on earth in truth! It is hard to picture in one's mind this silvery torrent befouled by bloodstains, these moss-decked boulders besmirched by battered brains and mangled limbs, the harmonious silence of this whispering, sighing, verdant wilderness, to whose beauty the roar of the cascade tunes ceaselessly fitting music, turned to discord by oaths and curses and screams of rage and pain, the baying of hounds and the rattle of musketry.

Captain Stoddart's track was afterwards converted into a permanent road, traces of which are still in existence and used by the hog hunters living about the villages of Somerset and Rose Hall in the Upper Blue Mountain Valley in the Parish of St. Thomas. But they are always careful only to approach within a respectful distance of Nanny Town; while the Maroons confidently assert that none but themselves can go thither, and persistently refuse to believe that the writer of this description depicts the scene from his own personal observation. In fact, so great is their dread, that it is beyond question that there are now only a very few of the older men of the Moore Town settlement who know the place, none of the younger generation having ever been near it. Should this description and the legend attached to the spot arouse the curiosity of any traveller to verify for himself the story of spook and goblin, an application to the writer of this will put him in the way of doing it without any reference to Maroons.

So much for the historical and the sentimental aspect of the beautiful Blue Mountains, in wandering among which it will be strange if the words of Longfellow do not occur to the lover of nature.

" This is the forest primeval ; the murmuring cedar and yacca
" Bearded with moss, and garments green, indistinct in the twilight,
" Stand like Druids of old with voices sad and prophetic,
" Stand like harpers hoar with beards that rest on their bosoms.
        *   *   *   *   *   *   *   *   *   *
" This is the forest primeval, but where are the hearts that beneath it,
" Leap like the roe when he hears in the woodland the voice of the huntsman ?"

THE CLIMATE OF JAMAICA.

B Y the kind permission of the publishers, Messrs. Wm. Wood & Co., New York, we reprint the following extracts from an article on the Climatology of Jamaica, by Dr. Thomas L. Stedman, of New York City, which forms part of Buck's "Reference Hand-book of the Medical Sciences." Apart from the fact that the opinions here expressed are those of an experienced and competent medical man, they have a value of their own, as far as Jamaica is concerned, in that they are the deliberate and well-weighed utterances of one who is neither a native of, nor a resident in, this colony, and whose words may therefore be regarded as being untinged by prejudice and unbiased by patriotism.

Dr. Stedman writes :—It is difficult in a brief article of this nature to describe satisfactorily the climate of Jamaica, as owing to the diversity of elevation and other causes it varies greatly in different parts of the Island ; in some districts it is hot, in others temperate and even cool ; in some it is dry, others the rainfall is very great ; indeed, the only characteristic common to all the varying climates of Jamaica is equability. Thus at the seacoast the average temperature is 78° F., (the extreme range for the year being only 35°), while on the mountains at an elevation of between 4,000 and 5,000 feet the mercury ranges between 50° and 70°, occasionally falling, on the summit of the highest peak and in mid-winter, even to the freezing point. In the accompanying charts, compiled from the official figures in the "Hand-book of Jamaica," the mean temperature is given for the city of Kingston, and this may be regarded as the mean maximum for the entire Island. Unfortunately systematic observations of the variations of temperature in the more elevated portions of the interior are wanting, but numerous unofficial readings of ordinary thermometers, taken with more or less regularity for a number of years by private individuals, show that the in-door temperature in places in the interior is on an average from 5 to 15° below the figures here given. From June, 1880, to the end of the year 1886, the readings of the thermometer were taken at eight hour intervals, to wit, at 7 A. M. and at 3 and 11 P. M., but since that time at 7 A. M. and 3 P. M. only. During the entire period the highest temperature observed was 96.1°, recorded on September 12th, 1890, and the lowest was 56.7°, recorded on December 4th, 1887. The *absolute* maxima and minima are not given in the first table, but their averages are about four degrees above and below the maxima and minima deduced from the daily readings.

The most striking peculiarity of the climate of Jamaica is its variety combined with equability. A ride of a few miles into the hills will bring one from the torrid zone to the temperate—from an average temperature of nearly 80° to one of 65° or 70°. But whatever district one may select, whether a warm one or a cool one, he will find the temperature very nearly constant, the extreme range for any one month being seldom over 25° Fahrenheit, while that for the entire year, at Kingston, is but 35°; and in some parts of the Island the excursions of the mercury are even more restricted than this. As regards humidity, also, there is the same choice of climate open to the invalid or the pleasure seeker, who may select a place of residence with a humid or a dry atmosphere as suits best his inclinations or the necessities of

FERRY ON RIO COBRE RIVER.

the affection from which he suffers. Jamaica indeed enjoys all the advantages in respect to uniformity of temperature of island climates in general, while the differences in elevation and in exposure to, or protection from the prevailing trade winds give to it the pleasing diversity, as regards temperature, humidity, and rainfall of the most temperate of continental climates.

In the first of the meteorological charts the rainfall is given in two columns, one for Kingston and the other, the average for the whole Island. There is, as a rule, less rain in Kingston than in most of the other parts of the Island, the trade winds being drained of their moisture by the mountains to the north and east of the city. The heaviest precipitation occurs in the Parish of Portland which forms the northeastern extremity of the Island.

METEOROLOGICAL CHARTS FOR THE CITY OF KINGSTON, JAMAICA.

(Compiled by MAXWELL HALL, M. A., F. R. A. S., F. R. M. S.)

For the Ten Years from June, 1880, to May, 1890.

Month	Barom. Pressure (In.)	Temperatures				Wind (S. E.), Miles per diem.	Cloud, percentage of whole sky.	Humidity	Rainfall	
		Mean	Maximum	Minimum	Range				Kingston (In.)	The Island (In.)
January	30.054	74.6	86.4	66.4	19.6	68	29	78	0.96	3.87
February	30.049	74.7	85.8	66.8	19.0	72	27	78	0.32	2.62
March	30.034	75.8	85.7	67.8	17.9	77	29	77	1.59	2.88
April	30.008	77.9	86.5	69.8	16.7	68	39	75	1.02	4.18
May	29.979	79.4	87.2	72.4	14.8	74	56	78	6.50	8.40
June	30.000	80.8	88.5	73.8	14.7	115	57	78	5.51	7.83
July	30.024	81.1	89.1	73.5	16.2	103	52	76	2.15	4.32
August	29.983	80.4	89.4	73.2	16.2	80	55	79	4.09	6.83
September	29.956	80.1	89.0	73.1	16.4	70	62	80	3.59	6.86
October	29.937	78.9	88.9	72.1	16.1	56	58	81	4.69	7.84
November	29.962	77.8	88.6	70.7	18.2	53	44	78	1.22	5.07
December	30.005	75.7	87.0	68.4	18.6	57	38	78	1.50	5.60
Means or Totals.	29.999	78.1	87.8	70.7	17.1	89	55	78	32.64	66.30

For the Year 1891.

Month	Mean Temperatures					Extremes of Temperature			Wind, Miles per diem.	Cloud, percentage of whole sky.		Humidity		Rainfall. (Kingston only.)
	7 a.m.	3 p.m.	Maximum	Minimum	Range	Maximum	Minimum	Range		7 a.m.	3 p.m.	7 a.m.	3 p.m.	In.
January	68.4	83.4	86.8	66.5	20.3	90.4	61.5	28.9	53.9	13	48	84	60	0.41
February	69.6	83.9	86.7	66.9	19.8	90.2	63.6	26.6	127.1	30	40	79	55	0.27
March	70.4	82.9	85.8	67.4	18.4	91.4	63.2	28.2	73.5	25	42	80	59	0.04
April	74.9	84.6	86.3	71.9	14.4	89.1	68.4	20.7	70.0	31	53	78	61	1.25
May	77.1	85.2	87.0	73.1	13.9	91.0	69.9	21.1	63.5	48	63	78	63	2.03
June	79.0	85.9	87.7	74.9	12.8	90.9	72.2	18.7	112.7	50	74	76	65	6.47
July	78.6	88.6	90.4	75.0	15.4	96.1	72.0	24.1	116.7	38	62	72	56	0.49
August	76.8	85.6	91.2	74.5	16.7	96.0	70.0	26.7	69.8	44	74	79	66	3.08
September	76.9	85.6	89.6	74.4	15.0	91.0	70.5	21.2	41.6	56	84	80	69	1.54
October	75.6	83.2	87.1	74.0	13.1	91.1	70.1	21.4	77.8	74	90	84	71	9.10
November	72.7	83.6	84.1	69.3	14.8	88.9	66.0	23.0	63.1	36	68	88	66	3.95
December	69.8	84.0	87.1	69.4	17.7	89.3	63.0	25.4	77.1	23	61	83	59	0.23
Means or Totals.	74.1	84.7	87.5	71.5	16.0	91.5	67.7	23.8	78.4	39	63	80	62	28.86

There are two principal rainy seasons, namely in May and October, but there is usually more or less rain all through the summer months. In the winter months in the neighbourhood of Kingston the precipitation is very light. The rain usually comes in heavy showers of only a few hours' duration, and the days during which the sun does not shine at all are very rare. It is almost always possible to predict when the rain is coming as it can be seen, quite a while

AVENUE OF COTTON TREES.

before its arrival, advancing from the mountains, giving one ample time to get under cover before the downpour begins. This is fortunate for the visitor, as a wetting is one of the three things that an unacclimated person in the tropics must avoid, the other two being exposure to the direct rays of the noonday sun and to the cool night air.

MINERAL SPRINGS OF JAMAICA.

ONE PINT CONTAINS :	Milk River Bath. (Analysis by Sarony & Moore.)	St. Thomas the Apostle. (Analysis by Bowrey.)	Jamaica Spa. (Analysis by E. Turner.)	Silver Hill Spring. (Analysis by Bowrey.)	Manatee Bay Spring.
	Grains.	Grains.	Grains.	Grains.	Grains.
Carbonate of Sodium	—	0.21	—	—	
Carbonate of Iron	—	—	—	—	traces
Carbonate of Calcium	—	—	0.866	—	2.71
Chloride of Potassium	1.44	0.04	—	—	—
Chloride of Magnesium	37.08	—	—	—	4.34
Chloride of Sodium	186.93	1.48	—	0.125	52.52
Chloride of Calcium	13.50	—	—	—	1.31
Chloride of Lithium	traces	—	—	—	—
Sulphate of Sodium	27.93	0.79	—	0.341	—
Sulphate of Magnesium	—	—	2.831	1.745	—
Sulphate of Calcium	—	0.62	—	1.234	—
Sulphate of Iron	—	—	2.210	0.833	—
Sulphate of Aluminium	—	—	4.168	1.360	—
Phosphate of Aluminium	—	—	—	—	traces
Iodide of Sodium	traces	—	—	—	—
Bromide of Sodium	traces	—	—	—	—
Bromide of Potassium	traces	—	—	—	—
Bromide of Magnesium	traces	—	—	—	—
Silicate of Sodium	—	0.45	—	—	—
Silica	traces	—	—	0.883	—
Totals	266.88	3.59	10.073	6.521	60.88
Temperature (Fahrenheit)	92°	130°	63°		
Sulphuretted Hydrogen		Undetermined.			

The population of Jamaica, according to the census of 1891, is 639,491, an increase of about 60,000 since the census of 1881, and of 130,000 since that of 1871. The capital and chief city is Kingston, the largest and most important, as well as the healthiest, seaport town of the British West Indies. It is a city of 48,500 inhabitants, situated on gently sloping ground on the shores of a large and nearly landlocked harbour. The land on which the city lies is a gravel bed, and as it has a slope to the sea of about ninety feet to the mile the natural drainage is excellent. The water supply is drawn from two rivers at a distance of several miles from the city, and as regards freedom from contamination is above reproach.

THE SQUARE, MANDEVILLE.

The diseases for the climatic treatment of which Jamaica is particularly well suited are bronchitis, fibroid phthisis, incipient pulmonary tuberculosis, catarrhal affections of the respiratory passages, Bright's disease, rheumatism, various forms of dyspepsia, and nervous prostration. All parts of the Island are naturally not suitable for the treatment of all these varied affections, but for each one a locality exists where the patient can find the climate especially adapted to the necessities of his particular disease. Respiratory affections especially do well in this mild and equable climate, as may be judged from the records of one of the life insurance companies doing business on the Island, which show that the company lost but one life from diseases of the respiratory organs (bronchitis) during a period of thirty-five years. These do well in almost any part of the Island.

although there is even here a choice, as cases with scanty expectoration are most
benefited in those districts where there is considerable moisture in the atmosphere,
while those in which there is free or even profuse secretion are more quickly re-
lieved in the neighbourhood of Kingston where the humidity of the air is at a
minimum.   Patients with nervous prostration receive more benefit from a stay
near the seashore than they do in the uplands, and the same is in a measure
true of dyspeptics, especially of those in whom the gastric trouble is partly nervous in its origin.   Sufferers from Bright's disease do well, as a rule, in all parts
of the Island except possibly in the most elevated regions where in the winter
months the thermometer is apt to fall a little too low after the sun goes
down, and where, especially on the northern slope, there is at times a little too
much rain to be agreeable.   The same remarks will apply also in the case of

RIVERHEAD, STEWART TOWN.

rheumatic patients, but the latter would do well to take a course of the waters
at one of the numerous mineral springs, of which a few words may be said in
closing this article.

      There are several medicinal springs in Jamaica, some thermal and others
cold, which possess therapeutic properties of no little value, and which are
deserving of more careful study by balneologists than they have hitherto received. The most important of these, or at least the best known and the only
ones at which passable accommodations for visitors are as yet provided, are the
Bath of St. Thomas the Apostle, about a mile from the town of Bath in the
Parish of St. Thomas, the Jamaica Spa, at Silver Hill in St. Andrew's Parish,
and the Milk River Bath, at Vere in the Parish of Clarendon.   The first
of these is a thermal sulphur, the second a chalybeate, and the third a thermal
saline water.

      The accompanying table, extracted from a brochure on the "Mineral Springs of Jamaica'' written by the Hon. J. C. Phillippo, M. D., shows the results of analyses of these three and of two other springs on the Island. All of these are quite easily accessible from Kingston.

The limits of this article will not permit of a detailed description of each of these springs, but the subjoined analyses will suffice to indicate their general characteristics and to suggest their therapeutic application. The waters of one or the other of the springs are of value, taken internally and applied in the form of baths, in the treatment of rheumatism, gout, chronic bronchitis, catarrhal conditions of the stomach and intestines, constipation from abdominal plethora, hepatic and other congestions of the abdominal viscera, amenorrhoea, anæmia and chlorosis, various forms of skin diseases, and chronic malarial affections. The Government has made grants from time to time for the improvement and care of the buildings at these baths, but there is yet much to be desired in the matter of cuisine, bathing facilities, attendance, and other things that contribute to the comfort and entertainment of the invalid. In the absence of these desiderata they still possess the great advantage that they may be visited in the winter season when the more pretentious and better equipped spas in Europe and the United States are closed.

The best months in which to visit Jamaica are November to April inclusive, as these are the coolest and dryest of the year, but one accustomed to the fierce summer heats of our northern cities would find a grateful change in the hills of Jamaica even in mid-summer.

To the above opinion we may add. that a fair criterion of the healthiness, or otherwise, of the climate of Jamaica may be obtained from a study of the medico-military statistics of the colony. These are exhaustively treated of in an expansion of a paper read before the Jamaica Branch of the British Medical Association by the late Brigade-Surgeon S. E. Maunsell.

Beginning at 1817, about the time when a first attempt was made to compile statistics of disease and to classify under various heads the causes of non-efficiency among soldiers, Dr. Maunsell, in a statistical summary, shows, amongst others, the following remarkable figures :

YEARS.					RATIO PER 1,000,	
					Admissions to Hospital.	Fatal Cases.
1817—1836	-	-	-	-	- 1812.55	121.3
1838—1847	-	-	-	-	- 1526.66	63.07
1848—1859	-	-	-	-	- 1141.69	32.70
1860—1869	-	-	-	-	- 994.76	21.25

During the first of the above-mentioned four periods the soldiers were overcrowded in the enervating heat of the plains ; sanitation was almost unknown, ventilation was unheeded, water was collected from the roofs of the barracks whence it drained into tanks, it was never filtered and was too deficient in quantity to admit of ordinary cleanliness. And the other accompaniments of barrack-life were of the same type.

During the second period the strength of the military forces stationed in Jamaica was much reduced; hence there was more barrack-room accommodation and consequently a decreased mortality.

The reduction in the years 1848-1859 may largely be accounted for by the removal, first started indeed in 1842, of the European troops to Newcastle, 4,000 feet above the unhealthy stations and encampments on the plains.

The improvement in the decade, 1860-1869, would possibly have been more marked but for an outbreak of fever in 1867. This is a convenient place in which to pause briefly in our statistics, because one result of the 1867 epidemic was a War Office Commission, the giving effect to the recommendations of which has almost revolutionised the reputation of Jamaica as an unhealthy military station. This Commission plainly showed that in the zone, where yellow fever is endemic, an entire dependence on elevation as an absolute and certain safeguard was utterly insufficient, if it were accompanied by a neglect of other reasonable precautions which should be taken in every climate.

The above-quoted figures show that half a century ago three soldiers out of four stationed in Jamaica were twice a year in the hospital, and that twelve per cent. died every year. Other statistics, which need not be tabulated here, show that more than five-sixths of these fatal cases were caused by fevers, that on an average every soldier had twenty-three days of sickness during each year, each attack lasting on an average thirteen and one-half days.

We now turn to the military figures for the next two decades and we find :

YEARS.	Average Annual Deaths.	Ratio of Deaths per 1,000 Admissions to Hospital.
1870—1879 - - - -	5	13.77
1880—1889 - - - -	4	11.36

In the last-named of these years, 1889, the deaths from all causes were eight per thousand and from fevers *nil*.

Statistics such as these can have but one meaning which is that, when proper sanitary precautions are taken and due care is paid to personal hygiene, whether among military men or among civilians, the climate of Jamaica is as healthy as that of any part of the world. Admitting the possibility of contracting, through carelessness or otherwise, some tropical fever, this possibility is more than counter-balanced by the immunity from other sicknesses and ailments which have their origin, not in evil conditions and surroundings which man can remedy, but in the bleak cold of winter, in frost and ice, and snow and blizzard, against which there is for the delicate constitution no escape but flight.

ROYAL MAIL STEAM PACKET COMPANY'S STEAMSHIP "ORINOCO."

STATISTICAL INFORMATION ABOUT JAMAICA.

TO AND FROM JAMAICA.

THE Royal Mail Steam Packet Company, with its fleet of transatlantic and intercolonial ships puts Jamaica in fortnightly communication with Great Britain and with the West India Islands.

The Steamers of this Company afford favourable opportunities to persons desirous of taking trips for novelty, pleasure, or health.

The various routes include calls at places where the scenery is of great beauty and grandeur, and where the climate is warm and mild at the time when severe weather is experienced in more northerly latitudes.

The vessels of the Royal Mail Steam Packet Company are fitted with the electric light throughout and all modern improvements—Ladies' Saloons. Smoking Rooms, etc.. etc.

Passengers making pleasure trips in the West Indies can travel intercolonially by the Company's Steamers by paying a fixed charge of 25 – per day for each day they are on board, while at sea or in port, provided the time is not less than 14 consecutive days.

The transatlatic ships calling every alternate Friday are:

ATRATO,	- - - - - -	5140	registered tonnage.
ORINOCO,	- - - -	4434	" "
DON,	- - - - - -	4028	"
PARÁ,	- - - - -	4028	"
MEDWAY,	- - - - - -	3669	"

The West India and Pacific Steamship Company's steamers are despatched once a month from Liverpool, calling en route at St. Thomas, Port-au-Prince, Kingston and New Orleans. The Caribbean line runs direct between London and Jamaica ; the Pickford & Black's West Indies Steamship Line connects Jamaica with Halifax, Bermuda and Turks Island : while the Clyde line affords communication between Jamaica, London and Glasgow.

The main means of passenger communication between Kingston and the United States is by the Atlas Steamship Company, the New York offices of which are at 21 and 22 State street.

The fleet of the Atlas Line are all iron and steel screw steamships, constructed under the superintendence of the surveyors to English Lloyds and in accordance with the requirements of the British Board of Trade.

ATLAS COMPANY'S STEAMSHIP "ADIRONDACK."

The following particulars of the steamship "Adirondack" will fully describe the vessels comprising the Company's fleet as a great similarity exists in their construction, etc., etc.

The steel steamship "Adirondack," built in Glasgow by Aitken & Mansel, with engines and machinery by John and James Thomson, forms the latest addition to the fleet of the Atlas Steamship Company. The steamship is 310 feet long, and has an advantage for the comfort of passengers in possessing a beam of thirty-nine feet. The hull and framing are constructed of steel of a greater thickness than that required by the exacting requirements of the highest class in Lloyds. As an additional strength, she has two steel decks, the upper sheathed with wood, thus constituting the vessel into a steel girder of immense strength. For a considerable portion of the vessel's length the bottom is double, so that in the event of the outside hull being punctured the inner plating will effectually prevent water entering the main and vital portions of the vessel. She possesses fine lines, a sharp bow with clean entrance and a graceful, well moulded run. She has two masts, is fore and aft rigged, provided with "leg-of-mutton" sails, that are easily and readily handled. The hull is divided into eight distinct compartments by water-tight iron bulkheads, placed at intervals across the ship. The engines are of what is known as the triple expansion type, having three cylinders, any two of which can be worked independently in the event of a break-down. They are twenty-five inches by forty-two inches, representing 1,500 indicated horse-power. The boilers are of steel, three in number, and have Weir's patent feed heaters and patent feed evaporators. In order to avoid the disagreeable smells that usually emanate from the engine-room and hold, as well as to secure the position of least motion and best ventilation, the entire passenger accommodation has been located at the centre of the ship, forward of the engines, and above the main deck. The state-rooms, being on the upper deck, thus secure an all-around ventilation, with the ports so far above the water line as to seldom require closing; they are also unusually large and airy. The saloon is a steel house built over the state-rooms, with handsomely decorated stairways leading to the apartment.

Windows on all sides admit both air and light, in addition to enhanced facilities for pure air through a patent ventilating apparatus fixed in the ceiling. There are ample accommodations for over sixty first-class passengers. The saloon and state-rooms are lighted by electricity, each state-room being provided with a knob by which the light can be controlled at pleasure.

The Jamaica Coastal Service is performed by the Atlas Company's Branch Steamers "Arden" and "Adula"—the latter a recent addition to the Atlas fleet; both vessels were specially designed for the Island trade and are provided with all the latest improvements. The passenger accommodation is situated on the upper deck forward of the engines, the state-rooms being particularly large and airy and the saloons commodious and well appointed.

These two steamers, one of which is under contract to the Colonial Government, afford most attractive trips to tourists and give the opportunity of visiting some thirteen ports, each one surpassing the one preceding it in loveliness and beauty of situation; in fact, no more delightful voyage could possibly be suggested than this around the Island of Jamaica. It occupies but four days, through waters always smooth; and every few hours a fresh port is made where passengers may land, returning to the steamer, or, if they prefer it, journeying overland to meet her at another port. Frequent opportunities are also afforded in the same manner for the return overland to Kingston on horseback, or by conveyances which are always to be hired at reasonable prices at the various ports of call.

KING'S HOUSE AND GROUNDS.

SUGGESTED EXCURSIONS FROM KINGSTON.

ONE DAY.— To Hope Gardens; Gordon Town; Cane River Falls; Castleton Gardens; Port Henderson; Spanish Town; Newcastle.

TWO DAYS.—To Bog Walk, Linstead and Ewarton, sleeping at Rio Cobre Hotel, Spanish Town; Bath; Mandeville.

THREE DAYS.—To Mandeville; Moneague.

In all cases arrangements should be made beforehand both for lodging accommodation at hotel or boarding-house and for being met by buggy or carriage at the nearest railway station.

For excursions of more than three days' duration the tourist will do well to avail himself of the facilities offered by the Atlas Steamship Company, or by following any portion of the route round the Island which has been sketched elsewhere in these pages.

ACREAGE AND CULTIVATION.

The acreage of Jamaica consists in all of 3,692,587 acres. Of this in round figures 3,000,000 acres are available for cultivation of various kinds, the cultivation varying with the elevation above the sea-level of the latter number of acres, and nearly two-thirds, as shown by the returns of the revenue department, are in the possession of individuals or trusts. Thus there is room for fresh enterprise and increased colonisation.

LINSTEAD MARKET PLACE.

VARIETIES OF CULTIVATION.—Almost every kind of tropical and sub-tropical fruits has been grown successfully in Jamaica. The cultivation of many of these, such as tea, has not yet reached a point either in quantity or in quality, that it can be regarded as a marketable commodity. This may be largely due to want of capital to oppose existing competition or perhaps to the fact that other markets are more readily found for better-known Jamaica products.

The principal productions are coffee, pimento, ginger, cinchona on higher elevations; sugar, cacao, oranges, limes, tobacco, nutmegs, cocoanuts, pine-apples, bananas and other fruits on the lower. It has been successfully shown that Jamaica fruits can be preserved and made into jams and jellies, but as yet only a beginning has been made in the export of this species of manufacture. Fibre-yielding plants will grow in many places now apparently uncultivatable. As a winter vegetable garden for New York and other large American cities, Jamaica has hardly been seriously experimented on. While nature has done much, man has done little. Sugar and rum, once almost the only commodities largely exported, have been in recent years left behind by bananas, and there is no reason why other fruit industries, many of them requiring less capital and involving less risk than bananas, should not hold prominent rank in foreign markets. Industry, care and personal supervision of work bring their reward in the rich soil of Jamaica to an extent not exceeded in any other agricultural country.

GOING TO MARKET, JAMAICA.

POPULATION.

The estimated population of Jamaica at the present time is 660,000. An unusually large proportion of the people who in other countries and under other circumstances would form the labouring classes, occupy their own small settlements. This is partly owing to the facilities for acquiring land, partly to the cheapness of the bare necessaries of life and partly to man's natural love of independence and perhaps of indolence. Another reason, however, may be and probably is, the low rate of wages which obtains throughout the Island. Consequently labour—and especially good, skilled labour—is not to be had in any great abundance. This is an evil the remedy of which is too obvious to need mentioning here.